NEW
HISPANICS

NEW HISPANICS

THE NEW IMAGE
FOR
NEW LEADERS

BY EDWARD VALDEZ
AND
KIM VALDEZ, PH.D.

CEO INTERNATIONAL
AUSTIN, TEXAS

Copyright © 1994 by Edward Valdez and Kim Valdez

All rights reserved. No part of this book may be reproduced or utilized in any form or by any means, electronic, or mechanical, including photocopying, recording or by any information storage and retrieval system, without permission in writing from the Publisher. Inquiries should be addressed to Permissions Department, CEO International, P.O. Box 200902, Austin, Texas 78720-0902.

Library of Congress Catalog Card Number 94-069201

ISBN 1-886291-00-4

Printed in the United States of America

Table of Contents

Introduction 1

1. Image and Success 3
- Triumphs and trials 3
- Image vs. reality 5
- Overcoming stereotypes 6

2. What's Your Image? 8
- Working hard doesn't always take you to the top 8
- Your everyday image 9
- Ideal image inventory 10
- Know your strengths 11

3. Positioning 13
- Know your world 13
- Choose a Hispanic-friendly corporation 14
- What is your brand? 15

4. Develop Yourself 17
- It's time to upgrade 17
- In pursuit of excellence 18
- Life balance sheet 19
- Walk with mentors 20

5. Package Yourself 22
- If you are not Bill Gates 22
- Automatic pay-increase 23
- Fit or fat 24

6. Reengineering Your Wardrobe: For Men 26
- Plan your wardrobe 26
- Don't follow fashion; follow function 27
- Pay attention to details 29
- Looking good on casual Friday 30

7. For Ambitious Latinas 32
- Dress for success 32
- Advice from Coco Chanel 33
- Power from within 34

8. Do You Like the Person in the Mirror? 36
- Commanding presence 36
- 7,000 facial expressions 37
- Shave or make-up 38

9. Body Language and Gestures 40
- Power walk, power shake 40
- Do not touch 41
- Kick those nasty habits 41

10. How to Build Instant Rapport 43
- *Ki* 43
- Matching and mirroring 44
- Say what you mean 44

11. Speech Image 46
- Communicating across accents 46
- Are you listening 100 percent? 47
- Voice with impact 48

12. Conversational Image 50
- How to talk to everybody 50
- Are you interesting? 51
- Respect cultural diversity 52

13. 9 to 5 Communication 54
- American corporate culture 54
- Grapevine or gossip 55
- What do you mean "I can't write?" 56
- Effective telecommunication 58

14. Presentations and Public Speaking 60
- Know your audience 60
- Practice, practice, practice 61
- Anti-nervousness control 62
- Stand and deliver 63

15. Persuasion Secrets 65
  - Lessons from Jesus 65
  - Use slogans 66
  - Seven keys to influence 67

16. Marketing Yourself 69
  - Newton's PR strategy 69
  - The art of self-promotion 70
  - Visibility and publicity 71

17. Networking 73
  - The longest rolodex 73
  - Global networks start at home 74
  - Make others need you 75

18. Mind Your Manners 77
  - Etiquette: a ticket to success 77
  - Costly table manners 78
  - Act as an ambassador of Hispanics 79

19. From *Mañana* to Today 81
  - It's never too late to learn 81
  - Be true to yourself 82
  - Transform America 83

20. Invest in the Newer Hispanics 85
  - Learn more, earn more 85
  - Teach your children well 86
  - Encourage God's language 87
  - Help thy neighbor 89

Conclusion 91

Notes to Yourself 92

Appendix 1: Hispanic Achievers 95

Appendix 2: Suggested Reading 97

Programs 100

Introduction

The Hispanic Era is coming of age. Shortly after the year 2000, Hispanics will be the largest minority in the United States. Fortune 500 companies have already started giving attention to Hispanics because of our growing population. Hispanics in America have more buying power than Canadians do of U.S. products and services.

However, being leading consumers will not change the Hispanic socioeconomic status in America. Hispanic purchasing power will not change our image or status. Our personal power to become great will. As we contribute more to the economy, we deserve a better status in America. We must become leaders in America. We Hispanics must become self-actualizing individuals and full participants in America. To that end, each of us must examine what others think of us and what we think of ourselves.

Do others think of you as a leader?

Does your Hispanic image help your career rather than hinder it?

Are you getting the kind of recognition you deserve?

Can you honestly say you are fulfilling your potential?

If not, this book will help you.

Every day we are challenged by negative Hispanic images. Whether we call ourselves Latinos, Hispanics, Chicanos, or Americans, there tends to be one identity with Hispanic surnames. No matter how high a Hispanic rises in status or achievement, he faces some difficulty being identified by his success rather than by his background. Many Hispanic professionals have expressed that their Hispanic image limits their careers.

We cannot hope to become new leaders without positive images to navigate our journey. Now is the time to reengineer our image as new leaders who will make a difference for the future of America. All of us must work together toward the new image for New Hispanics, from victim to victor.

Through this book you will discover that you control your destiny. Make a commitment to re-discover the best in yourself. Take charge of your future by using a new course of action. This book will help you to design a road map to identify where you have been, where you are, and where you want to go in your career. Each chapter presents key strategies to help you transform yourself. You'll learn imagemaking principles from some of the most influential leaders in the world. The principles are not a luxury, but a necessity for you to succeed. The choice is yours.

Reading each principle will take you no more than 90 seconds. When you invest 90 seconds per day, you will suddenly realize you have the power to change your destiny. Things do not happen by chance, but by change. Apply each principle you read, commit it to memory, and reapply it.

Every so often a book is written that arrives at the right moment with the right message which changes the course of all that follows. We hope this book will mark the beginning of a new era in the hearts, minds, and lives of Hispanic men and women.

1
Image and Success

Triumphs and trials

Hispanics have come a long way. An ever-growing number of Hispanics have become leaders in business, politics, education, entertainment, and social service. Robert Goizueta, CEO of Coca-Cola Corporation, is among the top ten highest paid executives in corporate America. More and more Hispanics are occupying senior management positions. Two Hispanics are serving on the Cabinet in the Clinton Administration. More than 5,000 elected and appointed officials in America are Hispanics. Linda Ronstadt and Gloria Estefan are among the hottest selling female vocalists. Hispanics achieved a 41 percent increase in the number of Ph.D.'s between 1982 and 1992. César Chávez, the late founder of the United Farm Workers of America, won the Presidential Medal of Freedom. To paraphrase a memorable song from Gloria Estefan, Hispanics are "coming out of the dark."

However, these gains have not changed many Hispanic images in America. Consider what some people say about Hispanics. They say Hispanics:

- Are less intelligent.
- Are too emotional and hot-tempered.
- Are lazy and enjoy long *siestas*.
- Prefer to do things tomorrow.
- Cannot complete jobs on time.
- Are constantly late for appointments.
- Have big families and extended families.
- Consist of macho men and subservient women.
- Share the same culture.
- Are from poor backgrounds and live in certain areas.

- Eat rice and beans daily.

Unfortunately, these are the stereotypes of Hispanics. Despite many Hispanics' achievements, some appalling trends shadow the progress. A vast majority of Hispanics in the news are found in contexts of poor education, unemployment, crime, and poverty. Recent socioeconomic research findings still contain gloomy statistics:

- About 65 percent of Hispanics between 25 and 34 have either graduated with limited skills or dropped out of high school.
- About 3-5 million illegal Hispanics immigrants live in the U.S.
- Twenty-eight percent of Hispanics live below the poverty level (an increase of 30 percent from 1980).
- The Hispanic median income is just above $20,000 compared to the national median income of just above $30,000.
- Women are the single-parent head of household for 23.4 percent of Hispanic families.

In addition, a recent report by the National Council of La Raza stated that when Hispanics are shown on TV, they are cast as "poor, of low socioeconomic status and lazy," "failures," or as updated versions of "Hispanic banditos?" Pepe Serna, the star of the 1994 CBS summer series *Hotel Malibu*, agrees: "I've been in 40 feature films, 40 TV movies, 100 guest shots. 99 percent have been scumbags. I'm always killing or being killed, dealing drugs or something that's illegal."

These negative media portrayals and pessimistic research findings have conditioned people to believe that Hispanics belong to the lower classes and inferior groups. As a result, some people have come to believe that all Hispanics are poor and are draining the welfare system by having lots of children. Others perceive that all Hispanics are illegal immigrants and take their jobs away.

The challenge for Hispanic professionals is to develop their careers with the burden of these unfair stereotypes. A recently published book, *Voices of Diversity*, attests to the challenges Hispanics face. Many Hispanics are challenged by their managers' low expectations of their abilities. Some co-workers and superiors assume that Hispanics have minimal competence and that they are intellectually inferior. Some non-Hispanic bosses are surprised when a Hispanic worker does an excellent job or meets a deadline.

Hispanics are not the only ethnic group that faces stereotyping. We have images of non-Hispanics as they have of us. Even Hispanic sub-groups form images of each other. However, the Hispanic image is primarily negative in the U.S. and it prevents our success. It is time to change the image.

Image vs. reality

Your public image is what people conjure up when they think of you. Once you have a certain public image, it's hard to change it. The image is often based on either the first impression or a short interaction. Sometimes, your image is formed without any interaction. The image may be far from reality and may be unfair. Yet people react to your image, not to reality, because they don't know you or they don't have time to know you. For them, a fragment of the whole is your public image.

Image is often stronger than reality. In 1991, when the Mitsubishi Eclipse was selling against the Plymouth Laser in the U.S., the Eclipse was outselling the Laser 8 to 1 even though the two cars were identical. The only differences were their names and the companies selling them. At that time Americans had the image that the Japanese made better cars. Times have changed since then, and America has regained the automotive lead; yet it is the image that sells.

Your image determines how you are treated in the professional world. Your manager decides whether to promote you based on his perceptions of you, not on reality. He may not know you that well. Most managerial decisions are based on opinions, and managers are forced to form opinions of you on relatively few facts. Thus, being competent is not enough. Not everyone recognizes professional skills or looks for inner value. So if you think you're a person of integrity or competence, you'd better make sure you come across that way.

Your image can run your life if you are not careful. People tend to behave according to others' expectations, making those expectations self-fulfilling prophecies. They reinforce their images by repeating certain behaviors based on others' expectations. That reinforcement is great if their image is good. But if their image is negative, it becomes a vicious circle and may limit their professional and personal life. It's hard to break the mold. That's why Milan Kundera, the author of *The Unbearable Lightness of Being*, said: "A man is nothing but his image. As long as he lives with others, he cannot but be the person that others perceive him to be."

However, do not let any negative image control your life. Do not allow your past to dictate your future. You have the choice to reinvent your image. You can create your image to match reality. Furthermore, you can create a better reality for you and other Hispanics by managing a positive image of yourself.

Managing your image is not difficult or expensive. Ignoring it is definitely easier, but will carry negative consequences. Therefore, diligently work on your image. Learn how to control your image. Ensure what others see in you is positive. Take the advice from the 17th Century Spanish philosopher, Baltasar Gracian: "Things do not pass for what they are, but for what they seem. To excel and to know how to show it is to excel twice."

Overcoming stereotypes

The movie *Stand and Deliver* is based on a true story of predominantly Latino Garfield High School in Los Angeles in 1982. *Barrio* students who could not perform basic math had one person, Mr. Jaime Escalante, who believed that they were something more than their image. He told his students: "You already have two strikes against you — your name and your complexion. There are people who will assume you know less than you know because of those two things."

Escalante inspired students to dream and challenge both their stereotypes and other teachers' limited expectations. When they did well on their AP Calculus exam — better than students of other L.A. high schools — they were suspected of cheating and forced to retest. Even some of the students' teachers and parents thought they had cheated until all the students passed in the second test. This occurred 12 years ago, and the situation is not much better. For example, in a bank's training session, a Mexican-American employee was told by his instructor that she would be available for additional help. The instructor said nothing to other trainees who were recent immigrants from Asia and the Pacific Islands.

It is naive to think that people do not apply Hispanic stereotypes to you. You may think you can get away from them because you don't look Hispanic or are well-educated. Yet no matter how smart you are, whether you attended an Ivy League school, law school, or medical school or whether you hold a managerial position; some may think you got there because of affirmative action. Ruben Navarrette, Jr., the author of *A Darker Shade of Crimson*, had to suffer from the whispering of classmates as a Harvard University student. Stereotypes are alive and well anywhere you go.

Of course, Hispanics are not the only ones that suffer from stereotypes. Women and other minorities face them and still fight hard to overcome them. The degree to which each ethnic group experiences them differs in each situation.

The first task in overcoming stereotypes is to be aware of what others think of Hispanics. Then debunk the myths. Never succumb to negative stereotypes. Stereotypes will not limit you unless you let them. When Navarrette was applying to schools like Harvard, Yale, and Princeton, his high school principal advised him to apply to Fresno State University "just in case." He thanked him, but promptly disregarded his advice. With four years of hard work and perfect high school grades, he knew he was entitled to the best in higher education.

Don't try to change the image of the entire Hispanic population in America. Start with yourself and dispel the negativity. You can transform the Hispanic image in America one by one — by winning those who are close to you and moving beyond over time. "If it is to be, it is up to me."

Now is the time to help build the New Hispanic era. It's time to take action to become one of the New Hispanics. By reengineering your image, you'll become a new leader in business, in society, and in America. The following sections will show you how.

2
What's Your Image?

Working hard doesn't always take you to the top

Recently, Stroock, Stroock & Lavan, a prestigious national labor and employment law firm conducted interviews with 4,000 senior executives around the country. According to these interviews, promotion decisions are based on the following:

Formal Criteria	
Assignment performance	13%
Intelligence	12%
Diligence	10%
Knowledge of the marketplace	9%
Subtotal	44%

Informal Criteria	
Integrity	13%
Networking	12%
Personality	9%
Loyalty	8%
Office politics	7%
Exposure	5%
Others	2%
Subtotal	56%

Informal criteria, often very subjective, weighed more than formal criteria. That doesn't mean that it's not worth working hard; but you can't be assured that your hard work will lead to a promotion. As Michael W. Mercer, industrial psychologist, wrote to *Fortune* editors recently, "Being highly competent plus making a superb impression on the people who make or break your career can eventually get you $100,000 annually." Success takes hard work plus a favorable image.

Take a minute to rank yourself in each of these critical skills. Identify the skills you need to improve and write down how to improve.

	Excellent	Needs Improvement	Ways to Improve
Assignment performance			
Intelligence			
Diligence			
Knowledge of marketplace			
Integrity			
Networking			
Personality			
Loyalty			
Office politics			
Exposure			

Your everyday image

Corporate recruiters screen candidates by checking to see if the interviewee is the type of employee who would be accepted by their customers. The recruiters keep the likes and dislikes of the buyers and customers in mind as a checkpoint for accepting new hires.

What kind of impression do you give to your customers?

What does your boss think of you?

What do peers say about you behind your back?

How do your subordinates perceive you?

Have you ever wondered about these questions? If not, you may not have any idea what others think of you. Think of your peers. You may be surprised to find that you actually know more about others than you know about yourself. We all know someone in the office who could improve his image or reputation if he could improve one thing — e.g., his mannerisms, style, or voice. Then, what would be the one thing in your public image that others would expect you to improve? What would they say about your appearance, your walk, your talk, your voice, your communication style, your work habits, interpersonal relations, or manners? Are there any misperceptions?

Take time to write the images you think others have of you. They can be physical, emotional, social, spiritual, financial, and intellectual. Be objective and honest with yourself.

Examples	Your everyday image
too emotional	
confrontational	
lacking power	
nice	
energetic	

Ideal image inventory

The word "imagemaking" often has a negative connotation. When it is used in political campaigns, imagemaking has the connotation of covering up one's faults and weaknesses. Yet real imagemaking is the process of filling the gap between your present image and your ideal image. No matter how good your public image may be, you always have room for improvement.

Since you've done an inventory of your present image, let's get to know your ideal image; you can't improve yourself until you identify your ideal image.

What kind of image does your company expect of you?
- Each company or division requires different images of its employees.

What kind of image does your boss like to see in his or her subordinates?
- Some bosses want aggressive people and others prefer more cooperative ones.

What kind of image do you need to convey to progress within your firm?
- Observe the qualities of the people who are on the fast track.
- Study the characteristics of company heroes.

What kind of images would you like to project:
- To your clients?
- To your peers?

Remember that your ideal image may need to change depending on your target audience. Being flexible is the key to successful imagemaking.

Know your strengths

With your ideal image identified, you're in a good position to acknowledge your strengths. When you do a self-examination, it's very easy to be too critical. When you see the wide gap between the present and the ideal, you may feel like giving up because we all dread changes. That's why it's important to know your strengths.

John Vasconcellos, California Assemblyman, confessed that earlier in his life he had had a hard time accepting himself because of his strong Catholic-Latino background. From the day he was born, he was labeled as a sinner and had to think of himself as nothing. It was very difficult for him to break away from this mental picture.

The first step toward imagemaking is to accept yourself as you are. We were all created in His image, worthy of being called the children of God. Those who don't know their strengths lose hope and tend to give up. They don't have the courage to try or the courage to fail. Do not be afraid of failure. If you focus on failures, they will immobilize you with paralyzing fears. Do not be ashamed of failure. A failure is not a failure if you've learned a lesson.

Write down your achievements. (Don't trivialize your accomplishments.)

Recollect the things your friends praised about you. (For the first time, accept what good others say about you.)

Write down any good qualities you have in you even if others do not see them.

If you don't believe in yourself, nobody will believe in you. You can hold your head up even when others are trying to knock you down and blame things on you. Doubt your doubt. Most of all, doubt others' doubts about you.

3
Positioning

Know your world

Successful imagemaking requires fitting into your environment. To fit in, you have to understand your own culture. First and foremost, you are in America. While it's good to keep your Hispanic cultural identity, you can't be successful unless you learn to work in the North American culture (for details, refer to the Chapter 13). The most successful person in Cuba may not be the most successful in America. The most effective person in Mexico City may not be the most effective in Washington, D.C.

Despite cultural diversity, there are mainstream American values and assumptions that are a foundation to American corporate culture and the fabric of society. Here are two basic beliefs of American society:

- Everybody is "created equal."
- The individual has power.

The real picture of corporate America is:

- The world is still unfair. Promotions or job rewards are not always made on the basis of merit.
- White males still have an advantage. Hispanic representation on Fortune 1000 corporate boards of directors is less than 1 percent, compared to the Hispanic population of the U.S. which is more than 10 percent.
- If you want good things, you have to ask.
- Competition pays off. It is the survival of the fittest.

This does not imply that every Hispanic should assimilate into the American mainstream, but for those who ignore the basics, the price of not "fitting in" will be high. Don't be discouraged when things are not ideal. America is not a perfect country; the company who employs you is not a perfect company. Nevertheless, you have better opportunities for success in America than anywhere else in the world. America is a place you can dream the impossible dream and be all you can be. When you have a dream, no one can take it away from you.

In the end, don't be too comfortable in your Hispanic community. There are other cultures to know — including the American corporate culture. Seek other opportunities. In addition to adapting to the domestic changes in America, keep up with the global changes. The more aware you are of the world, the better the opportunities you will find.

Choose a Hispanic-friendly corporation

One of the most important decisions for Hispanic professionals is choosing the right company. Some companies will be better than others in fostering your professional growth and success. One Hispanic job candidate was told he did not fit the culture of the company to which he was applying. In a way, he was lucky to be told that up front. Otherwise, he would have spent years going nowhere, not understanding how he could improve to make a better impact.

Most minority professionals agree that corporations are doing a good job hiring minorities, but not at keeping or developing them. That's why it's important to choose a minority-friendly corporation. Lawrence Otis Graham identified such firms after conducting extensive interviews and a nationwide survey. His book, *The Best Companies for Minorities,* lists the companies that seek to recruit, train, and promote minorities. Some of the companies include AT&T, Chrysler, Coca-Cola, Eastman Kodak, HP, IBM, McDonald's, Motorola, UPS, and the Washington Post. The book provides Fortune 500 company profiles which include salary information, distribution of minority employees in management and executive positions, support programs, and corporate commitments to promote diversity in their employment practices.

You can use Otis' book as a guide in making an informed decision, but you have to make your own decision about the company that is best for you. Don't automatically eliminate a company on your list because it's not listed in the book. Look for potentials. You can bring change within a company and pave the road for success for other Hispanics.

If you select a company based on Hispanic friendliness, be aware of token companies. Some companies may give money to Hispanic organizations and functions for public relations efforts, but offer no more than that. Talk to the minority employees of the companies. Even within one company, different regions and divisions have different personnel policies. Remember to talk to people from the areas that interest you. It's as important as a formal interview.

Because of the growing number of Hispanics, companies need more people who have a Hispanic heritage and are bilingual. You can use the Hispanic demographic changes in America to your advantage.

What is your brand?

Do you know how much it would cost to make a product like you? According to an estimate by Mark Lino, an economist with the U.S. Department of Agriculture, couples with middle-class incomes of $32,000 to $54,100 may spend $231,100 to raise a child born in 1993 to the age of 18. And that doesn't include prenatal care, delivery, and college costs or costs to society. Considering inflation, you are worth at least $500,000 if you're in the 'baby boomer' generation.

We all know great products that failed in the marketplace because of wrong positioning or poor marketing; the public's awareness of those brands was low. That's why the first job of marketers and advertisers in launching a product or increasing market share is to study brand awareness. Smart people create their own unique brand in a crowded marketplace. They are remembered for that brand even after they retire or die.

The late Dr. Norman Vincent Peale's brand was a positive thinker. The late Jacqueline Kennedy Onassis used elegance and style as her brand. Mikhail Gorbachev, the son of a peasant, developed his brand as a new thinker and became Secretary of the former U.S.S.R. His new thinking, epitomized in *perestroika*, led to the new world order. Margaret Thatcher became the prime minister of Great Britain using her brand as an outsider. She was different from other members of Parliament: she was not from a prestigious family; and she was a housewife with children. The differences were not easy to overcome. Yet she used her difference as a selling point. Madonna's brand is being racy and outrageous. Despite controversies surrounding her, she sells millions of recordings and sells out her concerts.

Who is your target audience?

What is your brand?

What are your selling points?

What is your worth?

Decide whether you want to be a generalist or a specialist.
Determine whether you want to be an international or a local expert.
Observe whether you should play your ethnicity up or down.
Remember, your brand must reflect the environment and the time.

4

Develop Yourself

It's time to upgrade

Know when to change, the futurist and management guru Peter Drucker advised young people who wanted to become leaders for the next millennium. Most people resist change. But without the ability to change, you will soon become history. Credentials from the best schools or the best companies do not guarantee you permanent employment. One economist warned that those who have not updated their knowledge of technology by age 35 will become obsolete by age 40. Everyone is replaceable whether he is a CEO or an assembly line worker, unless he upgrades himself. The shift in the relationship between a corporation and its employees has changed from being employed to being employable. Those who do the latter constantly learn new skills and adapt to changing circumstances.

With corporate layoffs numbering more than 600,000 each year, employees have to think twice about their career plans. Many laid-off executives regretted that they had naively believed that the company was going to take care of them as long as they worked as hard as the person next to them. Settled in a comfort zone, they neglected to distinguish themselves.

In contrast, those who survived layoffs in the toughest circumstances had certain characteristics. A study of successful executives found that these people study industry trends every two to three years. They reevaluate their skills and knowledge and constantly upgrade themselves. They make themselves irreplaceable.

Do not rely on your company for your training. You must seek your own learning opportunities. Take charge of your career. Develop the competence to work with new or changing market requirements. Upgrade your knowledge and skills. Improve your attitudes toward your work. Get excited about your work every day. Each day is a new day to learn. It's another day to make a difference in someone's life with your products or services.

What are some ways you can upgrade yourself?

In pursuit of excellence

R. L. Jones wrote in *The Concept of Racism and Its Changing Reality*:

> Much of the expressed antagonism toward affirmative action is based on the belief that standards are lowered by allowing 'less qualified' minorities and women in entry positions ahead of more qualified white males. The historical fact is that minorities have had to be overqualified in order to obtain opportunities. An implication of the overqualification requirement is that, historically, white males have obtained positions with substantially weaker qualifications.
>
> Many minority workers feel that they must outperform white workers in order to advance. They also feel that they are penalized more for their mistakes than white employees. Why? White males still dominate the workplace. They set the cultural tone, the standards, and the criteria for advancement. In any given corporation, human beings are most likely to select people like themselves. People tend to choose the people whom they feel comfortable to work with or who resemble themselves. That's human nature.
>
> However, excellence is a deterrent to discrimination. Knowing that employers are most likely to select people like themselves shouldn't prevent you from pursuing excellence. To strive for less is to invite a life of compromise rather than one of conviction. "Show me someone with mediocrity," says Jonetta Cole, a black woman marked for greatness, "and I will show someone destined for failures."
>
> Of course, excellence will not guarantee you the job of your dreams, but poor performance will guarantee you early

retirement. Nothing excuses poor performance. Do not expect exceptional rules for minorities or people of color. Strive for excellence. Do better and do more than people expect from you. Your success and excellence will open doors for other Hispanics and minorities.

Success is a process, not a destination. The way to achieve long-term success is through small, daily, incremental improvements in each area of your life. When you commit to pursuing excellence in your personal, physical, social, and spiritual areas, you'll find the pursuit of professional excellence to be a natural outcome of your commitment.

List some ways you can commit to your pursuit of excellence.

Life balance sheet

Victor Kiam, CEO of Remington Corporation, developed a life balance sheet when he was a graduate student at Harvard Business School. An example is shown below:

Assets	Liabilities
foreign language abilities	weak at details
good health	poor finance background
strong network	unclear voice projection

What are your assets?

What are your liabilities?

The liabilities are the debts you must pay off. Make a goal to write off your debts one by one. Don't be overambitious by trying to do everything at once. Depending on your liabilities, it is reasonable to plan writing off one liability per month. Some may take years to turn into assets.

Make your goals manageable and measurable. If you are weak at details, double the effort to pay attention to details when you work on your project. Keep your balance sheet close to your desk as a reminder. Evaluate your progress at the end of each week.

When you plan to improve, don't focus on failing. If you think you can fail, you may fall into a trap. In *Leaders: The Strategies for Taking Charge*, Bennis and Nanus tell the story of the famous aerialist Karl Wallenda, who fell to his death in 1978 while walking a 75 ft. high wire in Puerto Rico. His wife recalled: "All Karl thought about for three months prior to his death was falling. It was the first time he's ever thought about it." After more interviews with successful leaders, Bennis and Nanus concluded Wallenda was virtually destined to failure when he poured his energies into not falling rather than walking the tightrope.

Don't think about the negative; just accentuate the positive. Use your energies to improve yourself rather than to fight the fears within.

Walk with mentors

Coca-Cola CEO Robert Goizueta had a mentor before becoming the most successful Hispanic business executive in America. The CEO of Coca-Cola who preceded him, Robert Woodruff, taught Goizueta how to become a leader. Like Goizueta, many high achievers attribute their success to their mentors. Mentors guide the lives and careers of juniors and pave the road for them. When times get rough, mentors get tough and help their protégés avoid building a case against themselves.

How can you find a mentor? Ask. Many people will be flattered to be asked to be a mentor for promising young people. Besides, those who have helped you will have more interest in your success.

Learn your mentor's style. Examine what he likes and dislikes, then become like him. Show your loyalty. Find the needs and fill them. When Goizueta was running for the top job, he endeared himself to Woodruff, then Chairman of Coca-Cola by arranging for the toilet in Coke's new headquarters to be identical to Woodruff's "throne" in the old building. Goizueta knew his boss hated change.

If you cannot find a mentor around you, identify the people whom you want to emulate. They don't have to be Hispanics; mentors and role models exist across cultures. According to Market Development Inc., the list of people most admired by U.S. Hispanics is dominated by American politicians, Catholic leaders, and Spanish-language entertainers. They include Bill and Hillary Clinton, Margaret Thatcher, Pope John Paul II, Mother Teresa, Madonna, and Julio Iglesias.

How about you? Whom do you admire most? Which of their qualities are worth emulating? Do not try to find a perfect example. You probably can't find a single person that has every quality. Nobody is perfect.

Write down your role models and their admirable qualities.

Name   **Qualities**

Visualize what you would be like if you had the admirable qualities you listed. Adopt those qualities as your own. Perhaps you can start by internalizing one quality per week.

If you insist on having a Hispanic role model, refer to Appendix 1, which lists Hispanic achievers according to their areas of accomplishment. If you still can't choose a role model, aim at becoming one yourself. When you become a mosaic of the qualities you admire most, you will make your life a masterpiece.

5
Package Yourself

If you are not Bill Gates

Bill Gates, founder of the software giant Microsoft, never had to fuss about his look because he is a genius and the undisputed innovator among leaders of Fortune 500 companies. If you have Gates' qualities, you don't need to worry about your appearance. But most people need to be conscious of their looks because the first impression is mostly determined by appearance. Dr. Albert Mehrabian of U.C.L.A. found that people judge others by:

Appearance	55%
Voice	38%
Words	7%

This study is not meant to discourage you from strengthening your vocabulary or expertise in your field. Yet it reveals that you cannot persuade others unless you master nonverbal communication. If others are not impressed with you at first glance, they may not pay attention to you or what you have to say. How long does it take to make an impression? Some say 5 seconds; others say 5 minutes. Either way, within moments of meeting someone, you'll make either a lasting impression or your last impression.

Margaret Thatcher, former Prime Minister of Britain, confessed that when she visited local governments as a prime minister, she judged an officer within 10 seconds and hardly changed her mind about the person after that. Then and there, she knew whether the person could get along with her.

One executive recruiter from New York mentioned: "Each recruit makes it or breaks it the minute he walks through the door for an interview. The initial impression is what will be the long lasting one. How one presents himself the first few seconds shows who he is and how well he has prepared himself."

You hardly get a second chance to make a first impression. In that brief moment of time, your eyes, face, body, and attitude convey who you are. You are the message. Thus, you should try everything you can to look and sound more appealing to others. As Spanish Jesuit and philosopher Baltasar Gracian said:

> Things pass for what they seem, not for what they are. Only rarely do people look into them, and many are satisfied with appearances. It isn't enough to be right if your face looks malicious and wrong.

What is invisible does not exist in the eyes of the beholder. A fine exterior can lead to a perfect interior.

Automatic pay-increase

A recent survey of nationwide salaries revealed that those who look better get paid 5-10 percent more than their counterparts. Those who looked pretty, handsome, or well-groomed were consistently paid more for the same job. In other research, a scholar sent two photos of each applicant — a plain one and one with a makeover — to two different companies. The companies who received the makeover pictures offered the candidates 8-20 percent higher salaries than the companies that received the plain pictures.

For the self-employed, having a good appearance can lead to easy loan approval. A Mexican immigrant who settled in San Diego became a restaurateur through hard work. When his son graduated from a state university, the son advised his father to borrow money to expand his business. He scoffed at the idea thinking nobody would lend money to a *campesino* [peasant] like him. But he did what his son suggested: dressed in his best suit, and accompanied his son to their bank. The bankers took them into a private room, served coffee, offered them cigars, and extended them a revolving line of credit for $100,000. With that, they opened up four more restaurants that year and four more the year after.

That's not all. You get better service when you look wealthy. Oprah Winfrey once did a show on how one's look affects the service one gets. She sent four people in ordinary clothes to expensive stores and clubs. They drove ordinary cars and had ordinary mannerisms. They were refused service by salespeople of luxury cars and fine jewelry; were given poor seating after long waits at four-star restaurants; and were refused entry into exclusive night clubs. When these same four people had makeovers, wore stylish clothes, and drove luxury cars, they acted as if they were wealthy and got better results. The salespeople, restaurant headwaiters, and night club bouncers were not only friendly but also anxious to get these patrons' business and have them return for more.

Don't you want to look your best? What would it take for you?

Fit or fat

A college department chairwoman wanted to apply for the deanship. Her mentor suggested she lose weight first before she could be taken seriously. That prejudice may not be fair, but it is reality. Look at the CEOs and executives featured in *Business Week* or *Fortune* magazine. You will be challenged to find anyone who is overweight or out of shape. Running a Fortune 500 business requires a lot of energy, something you lack if you're not fit.

Studies show minorities, excluding Asians, have more weight problems than whites. It's costly to be overweight. Fitness pays off and fatness pays. Overweight employees pay an average of $400 more per year for health coverage than those who are more fit. According to numerous studies, those who exercise three times a week and maintain good nutrition live longer, have fewer illnesses, and have a better quality of life than those who don't.

The traditional Hispanic diet often challenges our will to maintain a normal weight. Chips, avocados, cheese, beef, refried beans, and flan can be tasty, yet when eaten in large amounts can easily tip the scales. When the Center for Science in the Public Interest (CSPI) reported Mexican food as being fat-filled, many Mexican food lovers defended it. However, CSPI had some valid suggestions for making any Hispanic meal healthier:

- Reduce fatty cheeses (there are some tasty low fat or nonfat cheeses).
- Use less salt.
- Use leaner meat.
- Substitute low-fat sour cream or yogurt for regular.
- Use less oil in beans and rice.
- Avoid the use of lard.

Don't be defensive about your cooking. Even the French, who have been proud of their cuisine, have started using less oil and fat. The Mediterranean diet has captured interest recently because it emphasizes fruits, vegetables, spices, and grains over meats.

Choose health. Choose fitness. You'll increase your net worth.

6

Reengineering Your Wardrobe: For Men

Plan your wardrobe

Image consultants compare men's wardrobe planning to engineering. To have a good final product, a man needs good planning for a professional wardrobe. The planning principle goes like this:

Think of your suit as a photo frame and your shirt and tie as photos. The frames are expensive to change, but the photos are not. If you change the photo, the whole frame will look different. By changing your shirt or tie, you can create a different look every day. If you apply this principle with 3 suits, 10 shirts, and 12 ties, you can have 360 different looks (3 × 10 × 12). You will not have to wear the same combination for almost a year.

Planning will prevent you from buying something on impulse that doesn't match any of your clothes and may not be worn. If you have a limited budget for your wardrobe, start with a suit that has a solid color — either navy blue or gray. When the suit is simple, it's easier to choose variations of your shirts and ties. When the suit is intricate, you have limited choices in your shirts and ties. Here are some other tips in planning your wardrobe:

- Study the dress code of your company, written and unwritten. If there is none, look two levels up. Wear what your bosses wear, but don't overdress.
- Choose quality over quantity. Buy the most expensive suit that you can afford at that time. Well-made suits have a seamless match of patterns from the lapel to the jacket, the jacket to the sleeve, and the pockets to the jacket; it's the same for the

pocket pattern lining up with the pants' legs. Choose 100 percent wool or worsted wool for suits, 100 percent silk for ties, and 80-100 percent cotton for shirts.

- Be conservative. Deep, dark conservative colors convey a sense of power and presence like navy blue and charcoal gray. If you want to use colors, save them for non-business occasions or wait until you reach the top.
- Keep it simple. A man looks his best when he keeps his wardrobe simple; that's why most men look good in a black and white tuxedo. As a passionate Hispanic, you may want to shine, but looking dapper is best.

At last, don't forget your body type. Your clothing should match your body type. If you are too short or heavy, use the following guidelines.

Too short:
- Choose smooth fabrics.
- Wear matching colors for jacket and trousers.
- Choose suits with medium tones rather than very light or very dark colors.
- Wear trousers with a plain front rather than one that's pleated.
- Avoid a widespread collar unless your face is elongated.

Too heavy:
- Wear a natural shoulder instead of a padded one.
- Wear trousers a bit wider.
- Wear dark colors.
- Pick small patterns.
- Don't wear anything too tight.

Don't follow fashion; follow function

Your mailbox gets filled every month with catalogues offering the latest fashions for men on the move. Don't rush to order.

Don't fall for trends. Brooks Brothers in New York, whose clients include some of America's most rich and famous, carries the same styles they offered 150 years ago.

Clothing is more than covering for your body. You would hesitate to have a doctor in a T-shirt perform surgery on you. You wouldn't be impressed with an actor who plays a lawyer if he weren't dressed like a lawyer. Your clothing must fit your job function. Your clothing not only affects others' perceptions of you, but also your own mood and mannerisms. You wouldn't feel comfortable in casual clothing when you are expected to wear a suit. You would walk, talk, and act differently.

Clothing is particularly important for minorities. As John Molloy wrote in his best-selling book, *Dress for Success*, it is unfortunate but true that society has conditioned people to look upon blacks and Hispanics as belonging to the lower classes. Since he wrote the book almost twenty years ago, the images of both groups have improved. Nevertheless, the advice he has given to minority clients is still valuable: Dress conservatively; wear only those garments that are considered upper-middle class symbols — pinstripe suits, end-on-end blue shirts, Ivy League ties; and wear and carry only those accessories that convey the same message.

Even if you're on vacation, if you go to the office, you should look professional. After finishing a week-long cruise with his family, a marketing executive at a Fortune 100 firm stopped by his office to pick up some papers. While wearing his Docker shorts and tropical T-shirt, he was asked by a fellow employee, "Are you ready for the presentation?" He looked surprised and replied, "What presentation?" After he heard that visitors from the corporate office needed an update about a topic only he knew about, he decided to stay and give the pitch. Little did he know — until he entered — that it was his company's CEO and executive staff. After that incident, he always came to the office in professional attire, tie included. If you find that hard to do, keep a spare tie or two at work.

You should also respect your customer's dress code. Always dress as well as the people to whom you are selling. It is said that even Bill Gates had to rush to a department store from the airport to buy a tie when he was about to meet with IBM executives for the first time. Being a nonconformist, Gates didn't bring a tie. So if Bill Gates shows respect to his customers, you should too.

These requirements are not imposed on you because you are a Hispanic. They're imposed on anyone who wishes to climb the ladder in corporate America.

Pay attention to details

Do you look at yourself in a full-length mirror before you go out? Most men don't want to admit they look in the mirrors often because they're afraid to be considered too vain. What's the alternative? You can go through the day with an unbuttoned button, a zipper that's down, a missing belt loop, a stained tie, or some other shortcoming that's sure to attract attention of the wrong kind.

Every day at work you can find someone who's missing something in their attire. You can probably recall feeling awkward because you wore a wrinkled shirt, had a spot on a tie, or forgot to comb your hair. To ensure your best look, here's a head-to-toe checklist:

- Is your head or beard well-groomed and clean? Avoid hair products that make your hair look shiny or greasy.
- Are your clothes cleaned and pressed?
- Is everything buttoned and zipped?
- Is your tie underneath your collar and your shirt tucked in? For a good knot, a tie must have substance with inner lining.
- Does the tip of your tie reach the lower end of your belt buckle?
- Does your belt match your shoes and the belt loop size? A brown or black belt with a neat, simple metal buckle is best for business wear. The belt should not be more than 1 1/4 inches wide for business suits.
- Are your shoes polished, clean, and in good condition? Avoid multicolored shoes or those with high heels or platform soles.
- Do your socks match your trousers? Best materials are thin wool, cotton, and blends. Socks should never be very heavy or sheer.
- Are your accessories appropriate? The basic rule is: the less the better.

- Does your attaché look professional? A briefcase in good condition shows a more organized man. Buy real leather unless you are an animal rights advocate. A plain dark brown color is a good, conservative choice.
- Is your cologne worn modestly?

Answering yes each day to all of these questions will make you more productive. When you look clean, crisp, and credible, you feel great about yourself and are efficient all day long. Others will enjoy doing business with you.

Looking good on casual Friday

Apple Computer and Microsoft are among the first companies that introduced a casual dress code to their employees. In the beginning, outside company executives who visited these companies felt uncomfortable because even the executives wore no ties, jackets, or suits. Now more and more companies are replacing business suits with khakis and cotton culottes. General Dynamics' Tank Division and H.J. Heinz's World Headquarters have joined such companies as Allstate Insurance and PepsiCo in initiating a more casual dress code. They have given their employees a greater latitude for what can be worn to work. Many companies have included at least a casual Friday to develop a more relaxed, creative, and productive environment. According to the NPD group, a market research firm in New York, morale increases at least 60 percent when workers are allowed to dress more casually.

Yet dressing casually doesn't mean that you can wear whatever you like. A Hispanic professional complained that he couldn't wear a purple tie to work. Employers still expect employees to dress professionally. Bright colors for men are not considered professional. Being stylishly casual is different from flamboyantly casual. The quality of casual clothes is also important to your professional image. When you shop for casual clothes, buy 100 percent cotton pants and shirts. Avoid wearing jeans or polyester shirts.

Whether you're at work or at play, dressing for the occasion always helps. Never leave home dressed in a way that forces you to say to your client, "I don't normally look this way." You never know when you'll publicly meet a customer or one of your company's executives.

Style: don't leave home without it.

7
For Ambitious Latinas

Dress for success

If you walk around Wall Street in New York or Pennsylvania Avenue in Washington, D.C., you'll notice "seriously dressed" corporate women. To be taken seriously by their male peers, some women still choose to wear a gray suit, pink oxford blouse, and bow tie while carrying a bulky briefcase. Undoubtedly, pioneer corporate women's dress codes have helped women move up the corporate ladder. As more women break the glass ceiling, this serious look has been toned down. More women feel comfortable wearing a bright-colored suit or dress, but there's still something called "dress for success."

Whether you wear a suit or a dress, it should look both professional and flattering. The color, design, and cut should fit your job and status. If you're the only woman in a meeting, there are two ways you can dress. You can blend in with the male crowd with a navy or gray suit or stand out by wearing a bright-colored suit or dress. Your dress should look sharp and comfortable. One Latina professional said, "A woman should never wear anything she can't do the mambo in."

Even if you have gorgeous legs, don't wear a mini-skirt. Short, tight, and deep-cut clothes are simply impractical for the workplace. If you wore this type of clothing, you couldn't even pick up something from the floor. This is particularly important for Latinas who complain about the stereotyping of Hispanic women as "Latin bombshells." Avoid dresses that are too lacy or colorful; they are more appropriate for parties. These dresses can bring unwanted attention to your femininity and ethnicity; you don't want others to focus on your gender, but on your work.

Take care to look like a pro even if you are support staff. Don't wait until you're promoted to look professional. Without looking professional, you'll never get there. *Voices of Diversity* tells a story of a Puerto Rican who learned this lesson. Stella Rodriguez (a fictitious name) had been a bank teller in a Hispanic area for more than four years. Her performance had been excellent. When she saw a job opening in the downtown location, she asked her boss to recommend her. She was discouraged when she heard the one reason for her being overlooked: her dressing style. The boss thought that Stella's attire was too "flamboyant" for the downtown office. While the boss could have told Stella before it became an issue, Stella should have been aware of the professional dress code herself.

Look one or two levels up and observe how they dress. Wear clothes that are dry-cleaned or pressed. Choose clothes that will make you look efficient. Wear simple jewelry and accessories unless your are in the fashion industry. Watch the hairstyles of TV anchorwomen. Wear a hairstyle that makes you look like a pro. If you look professional, you'll have a better chance to be treated as such. Your work will be taken more seriously.

Advice from Coco Chanel

Coco Chanel, the world famous French designer, once said: "If a woman dresses poorly, people will remember her dress. If a woman dresses well, people will remember her."

You may think some people were born with better fashion sense than others, but it's not true. Fashion sense is learned, and you can learn it, too:

- First, you must know about your body type. Do not follow fashion. Not all "in" styles are for everybody. Some dresses may look good, but don't look good on you. Experiment with different styles. Try different designer lines to get to know your style.
- Second, you should know your color. Do not automatically buy your favorite color. There are other colors that may look better on you. Learn to coordinate colors. When you see fashion magazines or go shopping, see what colors are mixed and matched well. Play with different color combinations.
- Third, you must be disciplined. Don't buy clothes on impulse. Don't buy them because they're on sale. Don't buy anything that will make you look cheap.

You can also enhance your fashion sense through accessories. Accessories will give you a more complete look. They are also useful for expressing your personality. When you select accessories, consider the following factors:

- Your dress texture: Don't wear heavy accessories for light summer dresses or light accessories for heavy winter coats.
- Your figure: Big accessories for a petite woman can be overwhelming. Tiny accessories for a full-figured person are not appealing.
- The occasion: gaudy, dangling earrings are not appropriate for work. Never overdo it. Some outfits look better without many accessories because the dress already has a complicated design. Remember less is more.

When you package yourself, you cannot neglect your shoes and hose. Whenever possible, your shoe color should match your dress. Shoes must be polished, clean, and in good condition. Do not wear bright colored hose. Make sure there are no runs. Keep one pair in your office for an emergency.

A final comment on purses. Most men say they always wonder what is in a woman's purse. I solved the mystery when I had lunch with Susan Martinez (a fictitious name), a lawyer. When she opened her purse, I saw coins, store coupons, cosmetics, tissues, and dust. If her clients had seen it, they may doubt her ability to organize their cases. If you want to avoid this kind of embarrassment, don't open your purse in public. Instead, empty your purse at least once a week, then reorganize it.

Power from within

Do you remember how the world admired the late Jacqueline Kennedy Onassis? She charmed us with her grace, elegance, dignity, and mystery. She was a classic beauty, but most people will agree that the greatest source of her beauty was from within.

Two years ago, I went to an Elton John concert in Austin, Texas. On the stage, there were three female singers. One was thin, another was average, and the other had a rather full figure. Throughout the concert, I couldn't take my eyes off of the full-figured woman. At first glance, the other women looked better, but she seemed to have the joy of living. She was fully alive in her expression and singing. That made her the most beautiful.

Too many women are preoccupied with their weight and looks. Women are notorious for having a poor body image. Studies found female models had lower self-images than average looking men. Even the most beautiful women suffer from low self-esteem. Audrey Hepburn was said to have been self-conscious about her bony features when she was young. Some women set such a high standard of beauty that they are never pleased with themselves.

Beauty itself doesn't sustain women unless they nurture their inner strengths. The tragic story of Marilyn Monroe is a good example. As someone put it, "She had the beauty, but nothing else." Monroe didn't know her other strengths, much less how to nurture them.

If you want to have self-esteem, don't compare yourself with other women. There will always be better looking women than you are. Younger women are especially hard to compete with because youth itself can be power.

Don't try to be a woman you cannot be. Until recently, the standard for beauty was being North American. Enrique Fernandez, a fashion designer, suggests that Latina women don't have to look like North American beauties. You can be beautiful just because you are unique. Play up your strengths, says Maria Hinosoja, a National Public Radio journalist at WNBC and WNET. By playing up your strengths, you can make a masterpiece with what you've got. Barbra Streisand was not strikingly beautiful earlier in her career, yet she made her fans forget her nose by emphasizing other features.

Cultivate your inner spirit. Take time to get to know yourself. Latinas are too devoted to others and often neglect their own needs. Be good to yourself. Be generous to yourself. Do the things that will make you happy and beautiful. Remember, there will be no happiness at home unless you are happy. When you are happy, you will show radiance from within, and you will not only feel more beautiful, you'll look more beautiful.

8
Do You Like the Person in the Mirror?

Commanding presence

Every man I talked to wants to have a commanding presence. He wants to stand out when he enters a room full of people. But many feel shortchanged because they don't think they are born with a good physique. Some wish they were taller. Others wish they had a lighter complexion.

Think of a person who has had an impressive presence. What makes that presence? You will find that personality is one of the most important factors. Many people have charisma because of their personality, not because of their looks. Your self-confidence is more important than your height, weight, or physique. That is why Ralph Waldo Emerson said, "What you are speaks so loud that I cannot hear what you say."

Even if you're short, you can have a commanding presence. Napoleon Bonaparte, former emperor of France who revived its prestige in Europe, was only 5 ft. 6 inches. In fact, your height can be an advantage because people will constantly underestimate you. You can always talk louder and lower to compensate for smaller features. The late César Chávez was a small man, yet almost single-handedly organized a movement (the United Farm Workers) that challenged some of the largest corporations in the United States. Mikhail Baryshnikov is short, yet commanded significant presence whenever he was on stage because of his grace, agility, and charisma.

You can also appear authoritative and attractive through other inner qualities. Carlos Salinas de Gotari, President of Mexico, is bald, yet he has impressed world leaders with his political savvy and charisma. Mikhail Gorbachev, former President of the Soviet Union and another bald politician, impressed everyone he met with his serenity. Mother Teresa of Calcutta outshone everybody including the First Couple when she addressed congressional staff at the National Prayer Breakfast on February 3, 1994 in Washington, D.C. Despite her tiny figure and ailing body, she commanded respect with the presence emanating from her lifetime love for the poor and her devotion to God.

Create your presence by developing your inner abilities. You have to be confident to look confident. You have to feel comfortable with yourself. As political media advisor Roger Ailes said, "Charisma is the ability to never appear uncomfortable." If you still need help in creating professional presence, act as if you were Pope John Paul II or President Salinas. In an instant, you'll find yourself walking more confidently and those around you will feel your presence.

7,000 facial expressions

Abraham Lincoln said a man should be responsible for his face at the age of 40. The Japanese took Lincoln's advice and updated it for a new reality: "A man should be responsible for his face at 30." According to the Japanese, your image during the thirties will determine your career success and it will be too late if you want to change your face at 40. They're not talking about plastic surgery. They're talking about the face that reflects your life and spirit.

If you've been to your high school reunion, you can relate to this well. At your reunion, you saw totally different faces on the people you admired so much. Faces change according to what people think and how they live. As the Bible says:

> The heart of a man changes his countenance, either for good or for evil. The sign of a good heart is a cheerful countenance; withdrawn and perplexed is the laborious schemer. (Sirach 13: 24-25)

Thus, if you don't like your face, you can create a new face. Try a new spirit or different facial expression. Doctors say that facial muscles are capable of making more than 7,000 different expressions. Many executives are known for their poker faces. If you are one of them, stand in the mirror and think of the happiest moment in your life. Think of the saddest time. Watch how your face responds to each. As you do these exercises, your face will be able to express your feelings better. Don't fix your face with one boring look. You have another 6,999 expressions to choose from.

If you want a more smiling face, try to smile when you use the phone. You'll not only change your countenance, but also sound more pleasant because of your smile. You can also give a smile when you greet someone. You're likely to get a smile in return. Of course, your smile has to be genuine and sincere. And it must also fit the occasion. Some people smile or giggle to avoid awkward situations, but it can make them look less professional. When the former Gulf War hero, Norman Schwarzkopf, was 10, he had to choose a picture to be included in his class album. Between a smiling face and a serious look, he chose the latter. Asked why, he answered, "When I become a general, I want people to take me seriously." Even the 10-year-old boy knew that facial expressions must fit the situation.

Shave or make-up

Do you wear a beard or mustache? John Molloy advises all people of Spanish origin to avoid pencil line mustaches, because it triggers a negative reaction. Psychologists have found that men with beards were judged by others to be more dominant, mature, and independent than their clean-shaven counterparts. In contrast, clean-shaven men were perceived to be more friendly, trustworthy, and professional. Psychologists argue that a beard protruding from a man's chin emphasizes his jaw and exaggerates the size of his neck and head which intimidates his rivals.

If you want to try a clean-shaven look for a change, take advice from renowned fashion designer Egon Von Fürstenberg:

- Shave before your shower for a closer electric shave.
- Clean the head of the razor before you start.
- Press the razor against the skin in staccato strokes.
- Finish up with an overall sweeping movement.
- Clean your skin after shaving with a cold-water rinse or two.

- Massage gently with a skin-soothing emollient cream. If your skin is very oily, use an alcohol-based after shave.

Make-up is as important for women as shaving is for men. No professional wants to look like Tammy Baker. Having a natural look at work is best. After years of study, fashion consultant John Molloy came up with guidelines for professional women:

- If you are under 35, wear lipstick and little else. Do not use a lipstick color that stands out in any way.
- Obvious eye shadow is out.
- Long fingernails and false eyelashes are for actresses.
- Mascara must be used with great discretion.
- Keep your eyebrows as natural as possible.

You can be more daring for parties and outings. Consult with a cosmetician to choose good colors for you, but don't overdo it. If you want to emphasize your eyes, do not emphasize your lips. If you want to dramatize your lips, do not draw attention to your eyes. Author Philip Lopate says that glamour is the ability to recreate oneself as a mystery. Don't take away your mystery by wearing heavy make-up. Make-up should complement rather than cover-up your best features.

9
Body Language and Gestures

Power walk, power shake

Think of a few people you met recently who looked like winners. Did you notice their body language? They maintained good posture when walking, standing, or sitting. Their feet were firmly planted each time they touched the ground. They weren't afraid of standing tall. Some tall people, especially tall women, often slouch as if they don't feel comfortable with their height, which projects a negative image. According to Michael Korda, the author of *Success*, successful people walk with power even when they go to the restroom or to a water fountain. Their walk is intentionally paced, not rushed or slow.

You can also tell winners by their handshakes. Their handshakes are remembered even if they last no longer than 2-3 seconds because

- They shake firmly, but calmly.
- They maintain eye contact.
- Their handshakes are congruent with their voice, face, and body language.

Check yourself in the mirror and ensure your body language is friendly. In North America, direct, open, and eye-to-eye contact is perceived as honest and professional behavior. Pedro Sanchez (a fictitious name), an immigrant from Latin America, projected a negative image when he couldn't look his non-Hispanic manager straight in the eyes. The boss was 20 years older than he, so he wanted to show respect by avoiding his eyes. Interestingly, Latinas do not seem to have a problem with eye contact. Roger Axtell, the author of *Gestures*, observes that Hispanic women often hold eye contact longer than others, even with strangers, with the exception of Puerto Ricans, who avoid eye contact.

Don't worry about the level or age of the person you are addressing. Maintain regular eye contact while talking. Don't wink. It may send the wrong message. Winking normally signifies some shared secret, but it could also be taken as a rather bold, flirtatious gesture.

Do not touch

Hispanics are known for their hugging and touching. They give hugs and kisses on the cheeks to feel connected to others. This goes beyond family relationships and is still practiced to some extent in Latin American countries.

However, "when in Rome, do as the Romans do." In today's American corporate climate, it is better to be cautious. Touching and contact that comes naturally in Hispanic cultures could easily be construed as sexual harassment, especially when done to the opposite sex. Business contact is limited to a handshake and the occasional pat on the back. To give more than that would only invite misunderstanding. It's better to be nonexpressive until you discover what the norm is for your company.

You may want to give a hug to express special thanks, but verbal expression is enough. If you've known someone well and have already given hugs for a long time, you can continue to do so, but don't hug newcomers. Don't expect everyone to like your hug. Even people of the same gender may not feel comfortable being hugged. If you do give a hug in an appropriate context, it should last a split second without being too close.

Kick those nasty habits

Have you seen yourself in action on videotape? Most people are surprised to find distracting habits they didn't know. They include:
- touching nose, ears, or clothes.

- combing hair with fingers.
- biting nails or inner lips.
- clenching the jaw.
- fidgeting with legs, feet, arms, or hands.
- rocking in a chair.
- dry coughing when it's not needed.
- adjusting glasses.
- automatically crossing arms.
- smiling for no reason.
- laughing and giggling.
- rolling eyes.
- using lots of hand gestures when they're not needed.
- nodding to emphasize something.

These mannerisms can send wrong messages to others or distract your listeners. Fidgeting can be interpreted as a sign of nervousness. Using lots of hand gestures makes you look unorganized. Rolling the eyes is a fairly common gesture around the world and it suggests incredulity or amazement in some cultures. It's considered to be immature in the business world.

Whatever your body says nonverbally should match what you say verbally. This is the art of being congruent. Being congruent also means kicking the habits that don't serve you or others. People may not always remember what you say, but they'll remember what you do.

10
How to Build Instant Rapport

Ki

Have you ever met anyone you instantly liked? Perhaps it was someone you wanted to invite to a party. Or maybe it was someone you would like to get to know better. The person seemed to have ease and grace without even being strikingly handsome or beautiful. On the contrary, you may also know someone you instantly disliked. You didn't want to do anything with that person. What makes people be attracted to or repelled from each other?

In Asia, businessmen often check the *ki* of their business partners. They look for the people whose *ki* is in tune with their own in choosing a spouse, creating a team, or choosing a lawyer. What is *ki*? The Chinese character *ki* means air. While Westerners often mystify *ki*, it is simply the rhythm, spirit, or energy of a person that reflects the person's thoughts, feelings, and experiences. Therefore, if anyone want to change his *ki*, he can do so by changing his thoughts, feelings, and habits. That is, you can only demonstrate on the outside what you already have inside.

People like positive people. People want to know those who have positive energy instead of negative energy. If you want to attract positive people, you have to send positive energy to them. It's like telepathy. "Birds of a feather flock together." If you want to be liked, you should send out the mental signal "I like you." You must send the vibes you want the other party to feel. Attraction is often mutual. Nobody would want to meet someone who is depressed and pessimistic unless he is a counselor.

So control your *ki*. Keep it positive. Those who can control their *ki* can control their destiny.

Matching and mirroring

Top politicians and sales people have something in common: both have the skill of quickly establishing rapport with strangers and use it unconsciously. By matching some elements of others' communication styles (gestures, posture, voice qualities, or key words), they enter into a comfort zone of friendliness.

When they meet a person who talks fast, they talk fast. If a person has a loud resonant tone, they use the same tone in the rapport-building stage. They observe people's temperaments and adapt themselves accordingly. Former Soviet President Mikhail Gorbachev used his matching and mirroring technique and changed world history. When he met President Reagan for the summit, he acted like Reagan: a little loose and relaxed. When he met the "Iron Lady" Margaret Thatcher, he used her debating style. He knew she didn't need an ice-breaker before she got down to business. When he met the Pope for the first time, he made a confession that it had been a mistake that the Soviets had not taken religion seriously. He knew the Pope is used to listening to confessions. Pope John Paul II later recollected that the moment he met Gorbachev, he knew that history would be changed. By matching and mirroring, Gorbachev impressed each leader, became friends with them, and helped end communism in Eastern Europe.

So whether you're with a serious person or a jovial person, go with the flow and transform yourself. People like those who are like themselves.

Say what you mean

In this world of pretense, people can spot sincerity easily. People love compliments. Compliments invite conversation, but they must be sincere. False flattery will get you nowhere.

Don't say something because you think others would like to hear it. Find something that is genuine that they can believe. When you back your compliment with a reason (. . . and the reason I say that is . . .), it becomes even more credible. When you close a compliment with a question ("How is it that you are consistently able to negotiate so well?"), it can also provide a tone of sincerity. If you use compliments too often to everyone, your words will not be taken seriously. You'll be labeled as superficial.

Also avoid using superlatives. They distort the truth and cast doubt on your judgment. The common use of superlatives such as "superb," "phenomenal," or "fantastic" in daily conversation is a reflection of the American culture of dramatization and over-stimulation. People are not impressed with glitzy words anymore.

11
Speech Image

Communicating across accents

When former President Lyndon Johnson went to Washington, D.C. for the first time, he was embarrassed to speak because nobody spoke like him. His Texas drawl was an easy turn-off to sophisticated, Ivy-league-educated politicians and media people.

A language barrier is one of the most difficult to surmount. Despite efforts to value differences, people do not usually appreciate others' accents. Studies found "a widespread pattern of discrimination" against people with a foreign appearance or accent across a variety of industries in all areas of the nation.

When a person is hard to understand, the desire for conversation is reduced. Unclear pronunciation or poor grammar makes a speaker sound less intelligent. In that respect, some Hispanics are disadvantaged because English is a second language.

If people misunderstand you more often than you would like, be determined to improve. Don't take it personally when someone cannot understand you. The CBS Nightly News co-anchor, Connie Chung, a Chinese-American, had to improve her pronunciation and projection for more than seven years as a reporter even though she was born in this country. Many native broadcasters hire voice coaches to improve their diction as well. If you cannot afford a voice coach, listen to tapes for English pronunciation and diction.

Also try these suggestions:
- Slow down. Speak slowly and intentionally. It helps clear pronunciation.
- Avoid slang and colloquial expressions.

- Use basic vocabulary and keep it simple. It's not necessary to use technical jargon to impress your audience.
- If you're not sure of the meaning of a word or an expression, don't use it.
- Listen actively.
- Ask people to repeat themselves if you missed what was said. Don't pretend that you understand what you didn't hear or comprehend.
- Don't assume everybody means the same thing for a given word. If it's not clear, ask. There are no stupid questions when you're trying to clarify something.
- Repeat, rephrase, and illustrate messages and instructions. Even the best speakers need to repeat things three times to an audience before the message finally sinks in.

Are you listening 100 percent?

In one of the early stages of Southwest Airlines' flight attendant interview process, managers had each candidate give a five minute presentation to all other candidates and the hiring team. The hiring team monitored the interest level of candidates who were watching. Those who showed no interest to the presenter were removed from the short list. The management team used this process to identify team players. They reasoned that those who listen to others would be good team players and make better flight attendants.

Most people are not good at listening. They want to talk rather than listen. That's why people are pleasantly surprised when they meet someone who has exceptional listening skills.

A good listener is 100 percent present with another person. The listener gives undivided attention to the speaker, who feels special because of this experience. Many women have been able to marry their dream men by using their listening skills. The US Ambassador to France, Pamela Harriman, is one example. She married some of the most rich and famous men including

Winston Churchill's son. Her former lovers included Prince Aly Kahn and journalist Edward R. Morrow.

Christopher Ogden, the author of Harriman's biography, wrote that one of Pamela's most appealing qualities was her ability to listen well. She oversaw "every aspect of a man's life, boosting his ego, anticipating his every interest, convincing him that her time with him was the greatest thing that had happened since the juxtaposition of the planets." It's interesting that even the most powerful men feel their egos boosted when they have the undivided attention of the women they admire.

Even if you're not interested in getting the spouse of your dreams, listening is a critical skill to practice. It can win customers. It can increase your sales. If you want to be heard, you must listen to others. We have two ears and only one mouth, so a good rule of thumb is to listen twice as much as you speak. Here are some other tips to help you become a better listener:

- Hold your judgment. Relax and clear your mind so that you can be receptive to the speaker.
- Stay open to new information.
- Don't be distracted with the speaker's dress or mannerisms. Don't tune yourself out just because you don't like the speaker's looks or general demeanor.
- Keep your eyes on the speaker. Show interest by nodding your head or maintaining normal eye contact.
- Verbally acknowledge that you're listening through your feedback.
- Hear what isn't said from nonverbal cues.
- React to the message content, not the form of expression.

Voice with impact

Voice volume, resonance, tone, diction, pitch, and pace is 38 percent of your first impression. An appealing voice is even more important if you do business over the phone because that's the only image your listener gets. As more and more calls are screened with voice mail, you must use your voice well so that your calls will be returned.

One study found that Hispanic students tend to talk louder than non-Hispanics. If those habits continue, Hispanic professionals will find themselves speaking loudest of all: successful professionals have a lower voice, not a louder voice. Think of the voices you remember: James Earl Jones' baritone voice of Darth Vader; Patrick Stewart as Captain Jean-Luc Picard in *Star Trek: The Next Generation*; and Ricardo Montalban's voice in car commercials. They all have lower voices.

Some people are lucky to be born with a good voice. Gloria Estefan and Linda Ronstadt were born with exceptional voices, yet they continue to practice to sound even better. You can refine your voice, too. When appropriate, lower your voice. Studies have shown that people with lower voices and deliberate diction give the impression of having greater authority. Do jaw exercises to moderate the volume of your voice by repeating "blah, blah, blah . . . " to the notes of "doe, ray, me . . . ."

Make sure that you end your sentences with a downward intonation in your voice rather than an upward one which signifies a question. Downward inflections signify certainty; upward ones, uncertainty. One more worthwhile exercise is to tune in to your favorite DJ or news anchor and repeat everything that is said in the way that you hear it. Whether it's an hour in the shower or during your commute to and from work, you'll find these to be precious moments in shaping your voice to have impact.

12
Conversational Image

How to talk to everybody

More than 40 percent of all Americans describe themselves as shy. They have a hard time striking up a conversation with a stranger. They feel uncomfortable talking to people they meet at a party or gathering. Is there any cure for shyness? The world famous image/speech consultant Dorothy Sarnoff interprets shyness as sh-I-I-I-I-I-ness: shy people are preoccupied with themselves when they're in public. They worry about what others think of them while most people are busy living their own lives. If you want to conquer your shyness, use the following suggestions at your next meeting:

- Be other-centered rather than self-centered. Forget about yourself and focus on the person you want to meet. People love to talk about their achievements, adventures, fond memories, hobbies, pets, etc. Newlyweds love to talk about how they met. Older people love to talk about their grandchildren.

- Ask the questions others will have fun responding to, such as the best vacation place they have been to or how they got interested in their hobbies.

- Don't worry about successful people being tired of talking about their achievements. Barbara Walters, the world renowned television interviewer, learned that even the most successful authors are almost never bored by praise and sincere questions about their work.

- Ask open-ended questions like who, when, what, where, how, and why questions. Closed questions (with yes/no answers) invite closure. Avoid asking too many questions. You don't want to make people feel as if they were being interviewed by a reporter.

- Make sure you listen actively. There is nothing more rude than looking bored just after you asked a question. When you listen carefully, you'll find something to respond to and keep the conversation rolling.
- Know when to move on. When the conversation winds down, excuse yourself by saying you want to meet another person or need a drink. When you want to make connections, it's important to use your time well.

Are you interesting?

Do you know people who are really boring? When you see them in the hall, you may feel like putting a bag over your head. They talk about themselves all the time. Their interests are narrow. They keep talking regardless of your response even when they don't have anything worthwhile to say.

How can you become more interesting? You must become more interested in other people, cultures, history, current affairs, and events. The former image/speech consultant to Ronald Reagan and George Bush, Roger Ailes, suggests that his clients use the 70/30 rule in their reading: 70 percent should be related to their job and 30 percent to the current interests of people.

Having a sense of humor can also make you more interesting. People like to be with people who make them laugh. The first step to having a sense of humor is to improve your ability to laugh at yourself. Franklin D. Roosevelt often joked about himself, his wife, and his dog. John F. Kennedy often made fun of himself for dependence on his father's money. Ronald Reagan used self-deprecating humor well in turning away attacks on him by saying he was "just an actor," too old, too radical, or too ideological. Those who laugh at themselves are liked because they don't take themselves too seriously.

Humor also makes the workplace more pleasant and employees more productive. Allen Klein, a leading jollytologist, uses the acronym L-A-U-G-H to remind employees of the importance of humor:

L Let go. You can't laugh until you let go of negative thoughts.
A Attitude. Change your attitude with laughter.
U You need to look for the humor around you instead of waiting for others to lift your spirits.
G Go do it! Turn aggravating situations into humorous ones. Most situations are not so bad that there is no humor in them.
H Hear humor and see humor all around you.

However, be sensible and sensitive. It's important to have good taste in your humor and jokes. Don't say anything that could be construed as offensive, such as racial, ethnic, or sexual jokes. Also use humor selectively because some people can't take jokes. For some people, life is too serious. It's also important to know when to joke. There is a right time for everything. People who joke all the time are hardly taken seriously. There are moments for wit or humor and times in which business means business. The bottom line is to take your work seriously without taking yourself seriously.

Respect cultural diversity

Some communication experts believe that conflict or misunderstanding in the workplace is caused by differences in gender, age, values, culture, socioeconomic background, and work roles of employees. To be effective in the changing world, you must target your words to different groups.

Three-quarters of America's workforce will be comprised of ethnic, foreign-born, or female employees by the year 2000. Your success will be determined by your ability to cultivate relationships with people who have a culture, gender, or native language other than your own. We live in a time in which the use of certain terms might be considered offensive. Anyone can make an issue about being called anything. Some people object to being called minorities or people of color. Some women do not appreciate being called gals, girls, honey, or ladies.

A special challenge is race-related words. No term seems to please all of the people all of the time. Even national publications have been at odds about how to refer to different ethnic groups.

For example, in referring to Spanish-surnamed groups, the *Wall Street Journal* uses "Hispanics." The *Los Angeles Times* uses "Latino," because "Hispanic" is considered pejorative, especially by the largest subsection of that community: Mexican-Americans.

So be prudent in your usage of language. You rarely know what kind of background or preference another person has. Don't make a hasty judgment of certain groups. Respect people as they are. Avoid adjectives that spotlight others. Use the language that is inclusive rather than exclusive. Even if you don't know what to call someone, you may be fine as long as you don't use derogatory terms.

Avoid racial remarks under any circumstances. I once attended a conference where a Hispanic speaker repeated *"Viva La Raza!"* to an ethnically diverse audience. This phrase means "Long Live the Race." It originated from the Chicano/Latino movements in the 1960s and 1970s. Although some Hispanics may continue to identify with it, it can be a divisive statement in mixed company. Respect others and they'll respect you.

13
9 to 5 Communication

American corporate culture

Imagine a working world in which *"Qué pasó?"* or *"Oye cómo va?"* were the greetings, a hug in addition to a handshake were expected, and a two hour lunch break would be the norm. Unfortunately, these things don't exist in corporate America. Most Hispanic professionals work in a distinctively North American corporate culture and have to learn the culture to succeed.

Non-Hispanic managers are often concerned about whether Hispanic employees fit into their corporate culture. As more corporations see benefits in choosing culturally diverse managers, aspiring Hispanics need to reexamine the norms of corporate culture in the U.S.:

- Speak up. If you don't, you will be considered inferior or cowardly. Do not wait until you have the most brilliant idea. Say what you think.

- Level with others. Telling it like it is and removing hidden agendas are seen as authentic and constructive behaviors. Confrontations that may look aggressive are a commonly accepted form of assertiveness.

- Follow the channel of communication. It is said that Hispanic managers tend to ignore the formal channels of communication. The norm, except for unusual circumstances, is to follow the hierarchy.

- Treat people professionally. Don't talk down to others. In America, even subordinates feel like equals among themselves and will resent being bossed around or dealt with as inferiors.

- Be competitive. A certain competitiveness is seen as constructive and healthy. You may be judged on how well you compete with your peers, or even with your collaborators. Learn what the limits are in your organization.

- Be a team player. Being a team player doesn't mean just doing your job. It means making suggestions and bringing solutions to your team's challenges. You need to strike a delicate balance between being a team player and being competitive depending on the norms of your group.
- Learn to promote fairness and equality. There are strict laws and standards that govern what one may say or do to members of the opposite sex and certain groups.
- Praise in public, criticize in private. Feedback and criticism are normal techniques for managing and developing others.
- Learn to take criticism. It is not intended to humiliate but to assist you to enhance your professional skills and performance. Welcome criticism.
- Respect female superiors. At some point in your career, you may have a female manager. She will expect you to receive directions and feedback from her as you would from any other professional.
- Take initiative. Superiors are supposed to be approachable at any time. You can ask them for feedback, but you may not ask them to do your work in normal business scenarios. You should always be in charge of your work.
- Don't expect *personalismo* (having everything personalized to you). Interpersonal relationships with superiors, peers, and subordinates are on a professional basis, not necessarily on a social basis.

Grapevine or gossip

Staying connected to the company grapevine is important to your success as a manager or employee. Often you can learn more about your company or job from the informal channels than you can from the formal ones such as reports, memos, and meetings. Smart executives use the grapevine to influence others and to get the job done.

Whether information comes from peers, mentors, secretaries, managers, or people outside your group or company, you must learn to recognize, analyze, and use the grapevine. The challenge is separating the useful bits from the useless gossip. It is often said that the grapevine acts without conscious direction or thought — that it will carry anything, anytime, anywhere. You should listen closely when a reliable source is:

- Talking about reorganization or changes in personnel.
- Mentioning recent management decisions that will affect you.
- Giving feedback about you from other people whom he knows.

On the other hand, it is better to excuse yourself from the conversation when another person is degrading the character or performance of another worker or making ethnic or offensive jokes.

Being part of the grapevine also means you are an informant, too. People tend to share information to those who have given them information. Tell people about what will affect them and what they want to know. However, you should be selective and discriminating when you transmit information. You don't want to spread rumors just to be considered part of the grapevine. There are better uses for your time than that. When you share information, use discretion in the timing and selection of the person. Plead ignorance when you need to. Otherwise you'll be spending an unnecessary amount of your time keeping others informed when, quite frankly, you have work to do.

What do you mean "I can't write?"

"What Do You Mean I Can't Write?" has been one of *Harvard Business Review's* ten most popular reprints since it was published in the May-June 1954 issue. According to the author, John Fielden, the revision after revision of drafts is often due to style rather than typos, factual misstatements, or poor format. What is style? It is the way something is said or done by a choice of words, sentences, and paragraph formats.

Style often communicates to readers more than the content of a message. A secretary had to frequently rewrite letters for her Hispanic boss. Her manager considered her style to be too dry, lacking the color and spice Latinos would like to see in writing. However, both the manager and secretary did not realize that style must be altered to suit the circumstances and must express the power positions of both the writer and the reader. Fielden recommends six styles for different situations:

- Forceful style: situations where the writer has the power to request actions in the form of orders or when the writer is saying "no" firmly but politely to a subordinate.
- Passive style: negative situations or situations where the writer is in a lower position than the reader.
- Personal style: conveying good-news or persuasive action-request situations.
- Impersonal style: negative situations or those in which you're conveying information. This is also used in technical and scientific writing.
- Colorful style: good-news situations or writing highly persuasive advertisements and sales letters.
- Less colorful style: ordinary business writing which blends the impersonal style with the passive style.

However, business writing does not end with choosing the right style for those whom English is a second language. Even if you have chosen the right style, poor grammar and misspelling can hinder the purpose of your writing "to get the job done." One manager of an international corporation revealed that the first screen he uses for prospective job candidates is reviewing each resume for typos. If it has one typo, he rejects it.

When it comes to professional writing, there is no excuse for misspelling and poor grammar. Nobody will condone your mistakes because you're not a native. If you want to be treated the same as any American, you are expected to write like a native. Use any tools (especially software) that are within your scope to screen for typos or grammatical errors. If you're working on a significant proposal or presentation, get a second or third pair of eyes to review it before submission. No matter how many times you have reviewed it, a fresh perspective always helps.

Strive to improve your writing. Refer to *The Elements of Style* by Strunk and White when you are in doubt. Learn from award-winning journalists by carefully reading such sources as the *Wall Street Journal, Fortune,* and *Business Week.* Emulate good writers. Learn to write with precision. Your efforts will be worth it.

Effective telecommunication

The telephone has become the most common communication tool in the country; nearly 99 percent of the population own one. Because most people have used phones throughout their lives, they don't even think about what to say before they use the phone. Yet organizing your thoughts before you make a call will help you communicate clearly and enhance your image. You don't have the advantage of looking at body language, so you must speak clearly and listen attentively to deliver and to get the real message. In addition, use the following guidelines.

Phone etiquette:
- When you call, tell the receiver your name and company.
- If you are soliciting information, let the person know how long it will take. Be accurate in your estimate.
- When you answer, sound professional.
- Never leave a negative voice mail.
- Limit your use of the cellular phone in public places.
- Limit the use of your speakerphone except for a group conference call.
- Make your voice mail informative and brief. Leave an option for the caller to speak to someone.

Another important form of office communication is electronic mail (e-mail). Executives admit it's easier to ignore an e-mail memo than it is to ignore a phone call. Because of that, e-mail can easily make the office impersonal. Peller Marion, an executive coach in San Francisco, set up e-mail etiquette rules when she coached a team of office managers who didn't get along.

E-mail etiquette:
- Answer all messages within 24 hours.
- Only send factual information.
- Use phone calls or a face-to-face meetings for any emotional topic.
- Do not write anything that will hamper your image when it's read by others.
- Do not send a joke unless it has an applicable lesson.

Modern office communication also requires fax etiquette and pager etiquette.

Fax etiquette:
- Do not send a fax longer than 10 pages.
- Do not use a company fax machine to receive personal information when it is shared by multiple users.

Pager etiquette:
- Use pagers with vibration options (rather than beepers).
- If you must use a beeper, turn it off during public performances.

14
Presentations and Public Speaking

Know your audience

Presentations have four elements starting with 'P' — Prepare, Practice, Perform, and Persuade. The first task in preparing your talk is to know your audience. You must check whether they are:

- young, old, or a range of ages?
- diverse (multi-ethnic) or homogeneous?
- professional or academic?
- informed on your topic or novices?
- required, volunteered, or paid to attend?
- conservative or liberal?
- dressed formally or informally?
- mostly American or international?
- dining during your speech or not dining at all?
- pressed for time or unhurried?

After you identify your audience, determine the one thing you want your audience to remember; that is your theme. You should then note your key points to support the theme and examples to get your point across. Dr. Robert Schuller is one of the most successful television ministers with his *Hour of Power* program. Each of his sermons is organized with a few points and each point is followed by a concrete example. The example is relevant, captivating, and memorable. He hardly looks at any text during his sermon because a note card with the theme and main points is enough to guide him.

When you prepare your talk, pay extra attention to your opening. The success of your speech will depend on how well the first five minutes are received. Most speakers agree that if they fail to grab the listeners' attention during the first five minutes, they lose the audience. Use a surprising statement, unusual statistics, interesting quote, or thought-provoking question for the opening. A speech does not have to be a monologue from you to the audience. By presenting a surprising statement or asking a question, you make them think about your theme. When they feel involved in your talk, it becomes two-way communication.

You can also start with a joke or self-deprecating humor. Make the audience relax and they will listen to you. In a speech given at the University of Texas at Austin, Henry Cisneros, then Mayor of San Antonio, started with a joke about his nose. He said that people often didn't remember his name, but they did remember his nose, calling him Henry Cisnose.

Avoid sexual jokes. Once I heard a prominent Hispanic judge speak at a banquet. He started with a sexual joke. Nobody appreciated it. Remember that your character will be determined by what you think is funny.

Practice, practice, practice

Practice makes your speech perfect. Practice in the room you are going to use if you have access to it. If you don't, rehearse with a video camera or in front of a mirror. When you practice, refine the following three areas:

- Gestures:

Use gestures which correspond to the size of your audience. Use big gestures for a big group, small gestures for a small group. Use gestures which support your message. If you talk about something big, give big gestures and vice versa. Anchor your hands firmly and without tension. Holding papers in shaky hands or clenching the podium would show that you are nervous.

- Facial expressions:

Your face should look enthusiastic. Nobody can be enthusiastic about a speaker who has a stoic face. A great teacher once said,

"Be like children." He knew what he was talking about. Children have energy. They have expression. They paint pictures with their words. They have fun talking. Why not do the same the next time you face an audience? If you can't go back to your childhood, talk as if you were talking to your favorite child. Don't talk down, but use a joyful face. Lighten up and your audience will be enlightened.

- Voice and tone:

When practicing you should also listen to or tape your voice. To avoid a monotone or almost robotic tone of voice, you should speak in a conversational tone, as if talking to each person in the audience, not lecturing. The reason why Ronald Reagan was called the "Great Communicator" was because he spoke to the audience as if he were talking to an individual.

Anti-nervousness control

Once you feel prepared, you must feel confident and relaxed before you present. However, many people fear public speaking more than death. If you have similar fears, here are five ways to control nervousness:

- Breathe well. Deep periodic breathing taps the relaxation response in your brain. Close your eyes and inhale and exhale slowly.

- Psych yourself up. Imagination is a powerful tool. Visualize performing well, being persuasive, and speaking clearly. Ignore negative thoughts.

- Love your audience. Many outstanding performers have a special ritual they use just before being introduced to the crowd which reminds them that they are there to please the audience. Singer-actress Mary Martin would stand in the wings of the stage before her performances and imagine facing the audience, then extend her arms and open hands toward them, and repeat "I love you, I love you, I love you." By the time she went out, she felt very much at home, feeling welcomed because she was singing for people she loved. When

done with sincerity and honesty, that tool can go a long way toward dissolving any nervousness.
- Don't be preoccupied with impressing your audience with your knowledge and wisdom. Be yourself and be human.
- If none of the above works, think of your audience as being more embarrassed than you are because some men forgot to shave and some women forgot to put on their lipstick.

Stand and deliver

Your image as a speaker starts from the moment you walk into the room. You must look like a speaker. You must be the best dressed person in the room. Walk calmly, stand confidently, and take deep breaths as you wait to be introduced. This is not the time to rearrange your notes. You should have them ready before you get there. This introductory time enables you to establish rapport with the audience. Listen to the introducer carefully as if you are acknowledging what is said. You may have something to respond to when you take the podium.

When the introduction is over, walk to the podium with energy, enthusiasm, and presence. According to a rumor, Ronald Reagan used to take the afternoon off the day before he had an important speech to make. He wanted to recharge himself. After his complete rest, the next day he walked to the podium with energy, almost hopping with zest. His apparent energy and youth erased the public's doubt that he would not be effective because of his age.

After you've made a favorable image at the podium, it's easy to get attention. Show your enthusiasm. Make your audience feel that you're glad to be with them. Sound like an expert. You're not there to waste their time. Maintain constant eye contact with the audience. If you have problems with your eye contact, direct your talk to the smiling faces in the audience or to those who nod; they are your allies. Pause periodically, especially after you ask the audience a question or tell them something to think about. It gives you a chance to catch your breath and the audience a chance to digest what you just gave them.

Respect the time limit, especially if your speech is before a meal or you're the last speaker of the day. As people get hungry, they will be less patient with long speeches. Besides, you want to leave them with the feeling that they want to hear more rather than the feeling that they've had enough. Close your speech with the same enthusiasm as the opening. Summarize your theme and points briefly; during closing, even distracted people will pay attention to you just to be polite.

15
Persuasion Secrets

Lessons from Jesus

One business executive joked that Jesus was the greatest salesman in the history of the world. With one product (the Bible), he had established branches (churches) all over the world and has been expanding business for the last 2,000 years. Why were his messages so persuasive? Why did people have to take action when Jesus spoke? Jesus knew how to persuade others.

- His messages were condensed.

Bruce Barton, the author of *The Man Nobody Knows*, observed that when Jesus spoke, "A single sentence grips your attention; three or four more tell the story; one or two more and the application is driven home." An advertising executive himself, Barton found that Jesus had used the modern advertising principle when no one ever heard of advertising.

- His language was simple.

He did not use jargon. Even a child could understand his messages. His illustrations were drawn from the common experiences of everyday life. Jesus used few qualifying words and no long ones.

- He used parables.

Jesus used many parables to effectively deliver his message. He used such parables as the sower, the mustard seed, and the yeast. People remember stories.

- He showed consuming sincerity.

When Jesus spoke, people knew he cared. Every word he uttered, Jesus spoke with love and compassion.

- He showed conviction.

People give more trust to those who speak with conviction than with hesitation. Jesus believed every word he said.

- He used repetition.

In the *New Testament*, similar lessons are repeated. Jesus knew the necessity for repetition. Some get the lesson during the first time, but others don't get it until they've heard the message a few more times. Repetition is a key to effective advertising.

Use slogans

If you were asked to fill in the blank to the following, could you do it?

It's the real thing, _____ is.
_____, it's not just for breakfast anymore.
_____ is thirst aid for that deep, down body thirst.
Just _____ it.

Modern American life is hectic. You don't have much time for anything, especially for being persuaded. Your attention span is short. That's why imagemakers had to create slogans, sound bites that would grab your attention. Sound bites have been used in political campaigns and media headlines. George Bush won the election with the slogan of striving for a "kinder, gentler nation." Advertisers use slogans to sell products. Executives use one-liners to share their vision. In a former COMDEX speech, Bill Gates used a slogan that summarized his vision: "information at your fingertips."

To communicate effectively, you must learn to use short phrases to make your point. Whether you speak or write, grab the attention of your audience with your own slogans or one-liners. Before you write a long memo or give a long talk, think of how your message can be summarized in one sentence. One-page memos used to be the standard for KISS (Keep It Simple, Stupid) followers. Now one page is considered too long. It should be a one-liner or a maximum of one paragraph. Long, boring memos are out; sound bites are in.

Seven keys to influence

Each moment in your business day you either influence others or are being influenced by them. In the groundbreaking book *Influence*, Dr. Robert Cialdini used a sociological and psychological approach to describe common tools of influence used in every day society. Yet there are other keys to influence that sales people, politicians, and others with the power to persuade use each and every day. Those who constantly influence others use what I call R BASICS (pronounced "our basics"). Using these keys will help you get what you want even without having authority.

R = Reciprocation. Scratch a person's back and he'll fell obligated to scratch yours. It is true that what goes around comes around. The Hare Krishnas built one of the most successful charities upon this principle.

B = Because. Psychological studies have shown that giving people a reason after you ask them to do something almost always makes them comply. "Could you let me cut in line to make copies *because* what I have is for a customer?" In many cases it doesn't matter what the reason is . . . and the reason I say that is *because* . . . .

A = Alternate Choice. Whether you're buying a car or presenting a proposal, this method represents the Law of Contrast: when given two choices, one will be picked. There is a difference between asking "Do you want a car now?" or "Which car do you like better, the crimson or the teal?" The latter assumes the sale, something which effective contract proposals also do.

S = Social Proof. When other people do something, it's easier to jump on the bandwagon. Movies advertise with quotes from reviewers. Companies advertise with quotes from satisfied customers. Products and programs live or die by endorsements. Just ask some kids; the reason they want NIKE sneakers is often because of Michael Jordan.

I = Interrupt. Interruptions redirect a person's attention. When you encounter a customer who got stuck in a particular groove of thinking, you could break him out of it by asking an off-the-wall question or using humor unexpectedly.

C = Consistent Commitment. Small yeses up front lead to the big "yes" of a commitment, contract, or key decision. In buying a car, the "yes" of interest leads to a "yes" on choosing models, to a "yes" of options on one model, to a "yes" of the purchase contract, and possibly to a "yes" on extended warranty. People don't like being inconsistent. If they say "yes" all along, 99 times out of 100 they'll say "yes" at the end.

S = Scarcity. "Limited time only," "Good for the first 100 customers," and "Coupon expires on . . . " are several phrases used in advertising. If there were a lot of items available for sale, there would be no need for urgency.

16

Marketing Yourself

Newton's PR strategy

Public relations (PR) professionals define public relations as the art and science of creating, altering, strengthening, or overcoming public opinion. Celebrities handle their public relations through their publicist, agent, or spokesperson. To create a certain image, they plant a story, appear on TV, or disappear from the media. It takes a specialist to maintain a positive public image. However, ordinary people cannot afford to hire a specialist. They have to handle their own public relations through effective communication. You may say that you are not a public person, yet we all have public images. Any communication that emanates from you has some element of public relations.

A key strategy for making public relations work for you is to understand Newton's Third Law of Motion: Every action has an equal and opposite reaction. This summarizes a basic PR principle. If you want others to speak well of you, you must start speaking well of others. Look around you. Those who criticize others hardly get praised by others. They tend to be cynical and grouchy. No one should give out false flattery to receive praise, but it is healthy to find something positive in others rather than being negative. When you are tempted to bad-mouth another person, remember what Og Mandino, the author of *The Greatest Salesman in the World*, advised:

When you want to gossip, bite your tongue.

When you praise someone, go to the top of your roof.

The art of self-promotion

If you were a product, how would you market yourself? This was a question asked of job candidates at Microsoft. If you were an interviewee, what would be your answer? In America, people believe in self-advancement. Self-advancement is the way to achieve corporate advancement and global advancement. You must be in charge of your career and promotional strategy if you expect to make a difference.

The first step toward advancement is to make a difference with your achievements. If you excel at what you do, you may not have to sell yourself. Your work stands out in the crowd. However, if you're the only one that knows about your success, you'll be in the same job for quite a while. A Hispanic engineer at a large corporation confessed at the 1994 Society of Hispanic Professional Engineers conference that if he could start his career again, he would blow his horn more loudly. When he started his career 15 years ago, he naively thought if he did a good job, he would be recognized. But most people in his firm, including his bosses, were too busy doing their own jobs and promoting themselves.

Tell the world how hard you are working, what accomplishments you have made, and how innovative you are. Research shows that people who talk about their work confidently and positively project favorable impressions toward others. Be optimistic and upbeat about yourself and your job. When you talk about yourself, do not forget about your team — your peers and subordinates. If you want to lead, you must be endorsed by your peers and subordinates as well. Using strategies like these can help ensure that others say positive things about you because they will repeat what they have heard. People often forget whom they heard something from, so what matters is hearing something positive.

So be your own PR agent. Act as if you were speaking for your client: yourself. Avoid the modesty trap. In corporate America, modesty can be equated with a lack of confidence. Do not make even a casual negative comment about yourself. Others may use it against you later. At the same time, use discretion in any way you communicate so that you won't appear to be naive.

Visibility and publicity

Madonna, who is called a PR genius of this century, constantly sought opportunities to present herself when she started her career. She visited nightclub managers and called music station DJs to market her songs and band. She knew that no matter how good a song may be, if nobody knows about it, that's the end of the song.

To market yourself, you have to be visible. I once heard a story about one of the most successful black entrepreneurs in the country. He started his career as a janitor. He worked really hard, but nobody noticed it. So he decided to wear a red shirt when all others were wearing blue. Only then did people start to notice how hardworking he was.

There are many ways to increase your visibility. You can start today:

- Lead a volunteer work team.
- Work on a project with high visibility.
- Send a memo with impact to the organization.
- Suggest solutions to problems.
- Join a professional organization.
- Speak at a local organization.
- Write an article for professional journals or local papers.

If you seek local or national publicity, learn how to use the media. Americans tend to believe what the media covers. Media appearances increase credibility. Media coverage also gives free advertising for the self-employed. Media people are always looking for new stories. Send a press release about yourself and your organization. Make your story interesting and newsworthy. Make your story timely. Timing is everything for the news business. Present it in an attractive manner. Use slogans or sound bites that people can remember.

You can also grant interviews for television, radio, or newspapers. Before you agree to an interview, ask what the reporter wants to talk about and do your homework. Once you have agreed, ask yourself, "What is the key message I want to deliver?" Read a book or two on how to deal with the media, or work with a media consultant. Never go into any interview unprepared. Reporters are trained to ask questions and you must be trained to answer them. As someone said, there can be a tiger within a reporter.

Like everything, be prudent in seeking visibility. Some people are constantly looking for visibility and photo opportunities. They go to all the functions where the top executives show up. They seek any opportunity to meet influential people. They volunteer to give them a ride. They give them a call as if they were buddies. They drop names. Soon the lackeys build a reputation: a negative one. Not all visibility is good. You've got to be visible for the right things, to the right people, at the right time.

17
Networking

The longest rolodex

A lot of successful men attribute their success to a long rolodex. According to market research, each person has 200 prospective customers. That means virtually anyone you meet has the potential to bring 200 customers to you. America is a big country, but when it comes to professional circles, it's a small world. Mathematicians have determined that there are no more than four people (connections) that separate you from any other stranger in the United States.

Yet you have to go out there and meet people. You don't invent a better mousetrap and expect people to come beating down your door to buy it. Join the local Chamber of Commerce or other professional organizations. Go to the places where your potential clients are likely to be. Take initiative to meet the type of people with whom you want to associate. They may give you the name of a person who would benefit from your business or someone whom you would benefit from knowing.

For successful networkers, even the most unlikely place is a place for networking. Anne Bowe, the author of *Is Your NET Working?*, was able to expand her speaking business after she exchanged business cards with a person she met in an elevator. The person invited her as a guest speaker to one of the conventions he was organizing. At the convention, she met many more people who were interested in having her as a guest speaker in their organizations.

Have your business card ready. Introduce yourself like a pro. Remember to get the other person's business card too. Some people write down information about the person on the back of the card so that they can use it for the next conversation. Some use a more sophisticated system such as a computerized rolodex.

Periodically review your rolodex. Stay in touch with the people in it. Give them a call. Invite them to a party. Send them interesting news clippings. Send a congratulatory note for a job well done. Connect people with each other. Above all, do business with them. They'll be loyal to you. Remember that keeping in touch with friends is as important as gaining new ones.

Global networks start at home

In an article on networking in *Black Enterprise*, Hispanic groups were notably missing. The article identified strong networks among the following groups:

- Irish in Boston
- Italians in Chicago
- Koreans in Los Angeles
- Chinese in San Francisco
- Blacks nationwide

Somehow, the article missed Cuban-Americans who have built a strong network in South Florida and beyond. However, we Hispanics must expand our network without clinging to nationalism. Some Hispanics have brought the "rugged individualism" that this country praises, but carried it to the nth degree. They prefer their affiliation of Cuban-American, Mexican-American, Puerto Rican-American, etc. and do not want to be associated with other Hispanics. That kind of attitude doesn't help our status in America.

We must network with other Hispanics for our own sake. Instead of focusing on differences, let us direct our attention to our common interests to improve our status in our country. We can still be proud of our country of origin.

The United States is the first universal nation. It is made up of more immigrants than any other country in the world. Unfortunately, a nationwide study found that almost half of every ethnic group dislikes other minorities and all ethnic groups dislike bigots. We cannot direct other groups' likes and dislikes, but we can eliminate our own biases toward other ethnic groups and expand our network. Hispanics have an opportunity to be the most open toward other immigrants. We can also be the first to appreciate differences within the Hispanic group or outside of it.

By being open-minded, we can make our network international. In a global economy and wireless environment, our network base can no longer be just our company or city. As more and more companies are going global from Asia to Latin America, they need global managers who have broad networks around the world. Therefore, we cannot settle for just doing our job and living in an isolated Hispanic-American community. We must seek opportunities to meet people from other countries, learn about other cultures, and expand our horizons. To move ahead in corporate America, we must be able to adapt quickly to different cultures. Our global citizenship starts at home.

Make others need you

It's not what you know, it's whom you know. In every business transaction, some have clout and others don't. Those with clout are the power brokers, the decision makers. Identifying the power brokers is a key to your ascent up the corporate ladder. It helps you implement your ideas and get more recognition from your company's leaders. It can also make a difference in getting and keeping your customers for life.

The key strategies for identifying and using power brokers are to:

- Ignore titles. Titles are deceptive when assessing clout. There are managers who are more powerful than directors depending on whom the managers know.

- Be observant. Susan RoAne, the author of *The Secrets of Savvy Networking*, encourages you to pay attention to whom your supervisor eats lunch with. Being observant at staff meetings and hall talks can also help you determine who has the power and who uses it.

- Join the winner. Determine whose career is on the move. If someone is offered a key assignment within your group, make sure you help or learn from that worker. Harvard's David

McClelland has proven that associating with successful people helps you to succeed, and that being with failures will drag you down.

Nevertheless, remember that networking is not always just meeting the powerful people and using them. Networking also means helping others. Successful networkers have supporters from all walks of life. Some of them became friends because others helped them. So when you have an opportunity to help others, help everyone you can without detracting from your job. Go the extra mile. Make other people depend on you. Help the people you don't like. Make people need you. People remember those who have helped them. They will be available when you need them. It's part of the law of reciprocation.

18
Mind Your Manners

Etiquette: a ticket to success

"The workplace is getting ruder," deplores an etiquette expert Letitia Baldrige. As organizations are getting leaner, overworked employees are getting meaner. Rudeness yields only scorn and annoyance. Even your office enemies should be treated with courtesy. It costs nothing to be polite.

The basis of etiquette is being considerate of other people. It is treating other people as you want to be treated. The book *Correct Manners: A Complete Handbook of Etiquette*, written in the late 1800s, is one of the best sources of the essence of etiquette. Some of the key points include:

- Never break an engagement of any nature. If you are compelled to do so, make an immediate apology either by note or in person.
- Be punctual, precise with payments, honest and thoughtful in all your transactions, whether with rich or poor people.
- Never look over the shoulders of one who is reading or intrude in a conversation into which you are not invited or expected to take part.
- Tell the truth at all times and in all places. It is better to have a reputation for truthfulness than one for wit, wisdom, or brilliance.
- Avoid making personal comments regarding a person's dress, manners, or habits. Be sure you are all right in these respects and you will find you have quite enough to manage.
- Always be thoughtful regarding the comfort and pleasure of others. Give the best seat in your room to a lady, an aged person, or an invalid.

- Ask no questions about the affairs of your friend unless he wants your advice. Then he will tell you all he desires to have you know.
- A true lady or gentlemen, one who is worthy of the name, will never disparage the other sex by word or deed.
- Always remember that a book which has been loaned to you is not yours to loan to someone else.
- Mention your wife or your husband with the greatest respect even in your most familiar references.
- If you have calls to make, see that you attend to them punctually. Your friends may reasonably think you slight them when you fail to do so.
- Be neat and careful in your dress, but take care not to overdress. The fop is almost as much of an abomination as the slovenly man.
- If wine or liquor is used on your table or in your presence, never urge others to use it against their own inclinations.

Costly table manners

Table manners can cost you your business. Recently I heard a story about the cost of dining habits. After a customer executive dined with another executive from a top tier supplier, the customer refused to do business with the supplier. The customer remarked, "I can't see myself doing business with someone with eating habits like that. To me, it reflects how he must be managing his division, so I want none of that." The potential supplier's executive had sloppy and excessive eating habits.

Even if you're not dining with executives all the time, learn how to eat properly. Every time you eat in a public place, somebody is watching you and making a judgment of your character. Here are some straightforward tips for dining with other professionals:

- Place your napkin on your lap as soon as you are seated. If you must leave, place your napkin on the table to the left of your place.

- Don't bring up serious business during meals unless your clients bring it up first. Wait until the coffee comes before talking shop.
- Don't gesture with your knife, fork, or spoon in your hand.
- When you are the guest, don't order the most expensive item.
- Don't order alcoholic drinks except when your clients want them.
- Women shouldn't consider business lunch as a date. It should be a "Dutch treat."

A few more points from Marjabelle Stewart, co-author of *Executive Etiquette in the New Workplace*:

- Stay open-minded when dining with people from other cultures. Eat what they serve.
- If you're the host, make guests feel comfortable. When an Asian guest drank out of a finger bowl at a White House function, then-President Bush took a sip himself out of his finger bowl.
- Don't fuss over your dietary needs. You're invited for the seat, not the food.

A final note is about cocktails. A cocktail is not a substitute for a meal. The purpose of a cocktail party is to network and meet people. However, you should be careful drinking on an empty stomach. If you're concerned about the possibility of embarrassing behavior, limit yourself to one alcoholic drink or have another beverage. Hold your glass in your left hand so that you can use your right hand for shakings hands. Avoid flirting and keep your interactions professional.

Act as an ambassador of Hispanics

You will be noticeable simply because you are Hispanic; your look or name tells the world you are Hispanic. Whether you like it or not, you represent Hispanics when you're in public. Thus, a single act or word can help or hinder the public's image of all Hispanics. If you are kind and generous, people will perceive Hispanics as kind and generous. If you are mean and rude, people will perceive all Hispanics as mean and rude. So

don't be casual about your daily encounters. Follow the suggestions below:
- Be courteous in your conversation.
- Give kind words to young people working at stores.
- Be generous in your judgment of others. Have compassion toward others.
- Express your gratitude to those who deserve it: garbage collector, policeman, mail courier, telemarketing representative, etc.
- Lift up everybody you encounter with encouraging words.
- Show your kindness to people around you.
- Open a door for older people.
- Give change to someone who is short of money.
- Help someone in need.
- Yield the right of way to others.
- Give more than you are expected to give.
- Leave generous tips to those who work on Fridays and holidays.
- Make a difference in someone's day.

As a Hispanic ambassador, you can spread your good spirit and help change your community. Be a good Samaritan. Build goodwill. Bring good news to your neighbors. Let others see the good side of humanity and the beauty of life through you. Act as if the whole world were watching you. Upgrade your actions one level and be polite wherever you are.

19

From *Mañana* to Today

It's never too late to learn

At the 1994 Society of Hispanic Professional Engineers conference, I was sitting next to an engineering student from California. At first, he looked like an average college junior. During our conversation, I found out that he is the father of a teenage son. He said that while he was working one day on an hourly wage in Florida, he realized that only education could enable him to escape from a life of hard labor. So he decided to go to college and applied for scholarships. The fact that he was already over 30 didn't bother him. He had *ganas* (desire). He was so enthusiastic about his life and education that nobody could tell his age. When he said "everything is so beautiful," everybody at the table felt happy for him. We all knew he would be successful when he graduated.

The number of college students between the age of 35 and 50 has increased fourfold since the 1980s. Regardless of your age, education can change your life and career. Education can enhance your family life. If you think the lack of formal education hinders your career, look for ways to pursue more education. Ten years from now, you don't want to find yourself saying, "If only I were 10 years younger."

You may be fearful of returning to school if you didn't do well at school when you were younger, but your motivation to succeed will help you become a better student. In fact, a lot of adult students who didn't like school at a younger age liked school so much when they returned that some even ended up getting doctorates. The baseball star Felipe Alou once said, "A fellow doesn't know how good he is until he really tries." You may have to delay gratification like buying a new car, but to achieve a high level of success you have to be willing to pay the price.

If you already have enough education or can't afford to go back to school, keep learning on the job. Successful people are lifelong learners. This is especially true if you are self-employed, because you have to be responsible for your own training. Seek ways that will increase your knowledge and skills. There are enormous learning opportunities in America. They include:

- university continuing education programs
- community college courses
- informal classes
- public seminars
- corporate training
- educational television
- books & tapes
- newspapers, magazines, newsletters, and
- professional organizations.

"*Mañana* is today!" was a slogan used by IMAGE, a group started by Tony Calderon in San Antonio. This roughly translates to "Now is the time." Don't put off doing something that will make your life better and your future brighter.

Be true to yourself

When you have a burning desire to succeed, it's easy to lose balance. Don't confine your definition of success to fame, wealth, or promotions. You can have everything materially but nothing emotionally because you don't have friends or family. When you don't have anyone with whom to share your success, it won't be as sweet as you think. To make your success more meaningful, you must constantly ask yourself:

- What is the nature of my world?
- Who am I in this world?
- What is my relationship to myself?
- What is my relationship to others?
- What is my relationship to God?

You also need to renew yourself everyday by reinforcing empowering beliefs daily:
- Awake with a joyful heart.
- Read inspirational messages every morning.
- Visualize the image you want to project for the day.
- Think of who you want to be, not just what you want to do.
- Determine to be better than yesterday.
- Treat every day as if it were your last day.
- Think positively about everything.
- Talk positively to yourself about yourself.
- Build others up.
- Reflect on the image you projected during work at the end of your day.
- Resolve to correct any shortfalls tomorrow.
- Close your day with gratitude.

Transform America

"The paradox of the Latino experience in the U.S. is that light-skinned anglicized Latinos can always escape into the melting pot," argues Linda Chavez, the author of *Out of the Barrio*. She added that like other people of color, some Hispanics try to be as white as possible. Assimilation is one way of adjusting into American society for many immigrants and minorities.

But there is a price for assimilation. Having studied black senior executives, Sharon Collins, a University of Illinois sociologist, observed many of them "consciously shed any remnants that would remind people that they were black." She continued, "Think of how much a black person has to sell of himself to try to get race not to matter. There is a toll. You have to ignore the insults. You have to ignore the natural loyalties. You have to ignore your past. In a sense, you have to just about deny yourself."

Moving up the economic ladder has cushioned some Hispanics against the blows of discrimination. Yet we have to press further to guarantee better conditions for all Hispanics. In fact, it's not a matter of fighting for Hispanic interests. It's fighting for more justice in America. African-Americans and women have progressed by pressuring for change. As one *New York Times* editor acknowledged, pressure works.

Therefore, let us not be ashamed of our Hispanic identity. Let us not close our eyes to discrimination. Let us become full participants in the democratic process of America. Let us transform America with our courage and heritage. Here are a few examples of Hispanic heritage to reinforce:

- Have a strong regard for family and kinship.
- Be gentle and considerate toward others.
- Be industrious and hard-working.
- Have an amalgam of buoyancy and sensuousness.
- Reflect passion, a spice for life, imagination, and dreaming.
- Frown on drinking and smoking.
- Enjoy lively, colorful music, art, and food.

20
Invest in the Newer Hispanics

Learn more, earn more

In 1994, the Census Bureau released a comparison of Americans' earnings relative to their educational levels. It found that people with advanced degrees had average earnings of $48,653 in 1992. In comparison, people with bachelor's degrees averaged $32,629 and high school graduates earned just $18,737. Thus, those with advanced degrees earn about 50 percent more than those with bachelor's degrees and 2 1/2 times that of high school graduates. Those with bachelor's degrees earn about 75 percent more than high school graduates. Education gives a startling opportunity for achieving a better life.

It's a sad reality that Hispanics' high school drop-out rate is so high: nearly 50 percent drop out. Is it that tough for parents to keep their children at school? Some parents discourage their children's education so that additional short-term income can be brought to the family by having them work. Of course, when you have a family-owned business, all family members must help to reduce costs. Other minority business owners often have their children assist them in their restaurants, gift shops, or grocery stores.

However, the bottom line is that education must come first. You must make your children's learning your top priority. Their grades should not suffer. Many Asian teenagers were able to get in Ivy League colleges or other top-ranked universities while they helped their family-owned businesses. Their parents sent a clear message: school work is their first priority.

Some parents don't realize the impact of their actions on their children. One family in El Paso prevented their daughter from attending MIT on a scholarship because they thought it was too far from their *familia* (family). A Hispanic female teacher at a public school in the Dallas/Ft. Worth area deplored that Hispanic moms often can't help their children because their fathers expect fresh tortillas everyday. The fathers get angry if the mothers volunteer at school and come home too late to make fresh tortillas. "The *'machismo'* attitude still predominates first, second, and third generation families that continue to live in a survival mode," said the teacher.

Hector Ruiz, Senior Vice President of Motorola's Paging Products Group, used to shine shoes for 5 cents as a 6 year old boy in Mexico. His career goal was to start his own auto repair shop. But his father made a deal: "Go to America for college. Try it for one year; if you still don't like it at the end of the year, I'll help you start your own shop." Since he didn't know English, he worked hard day and night studying with a dictionary in one hand. He found himself enjoying his education so much that he went on to get a Ph.D. Behind a successful businessman was an inspiring father who left a lifelong impact. Ruiz recalled with much sentiment when he repeated what his father had told him shortly before the birth of his son, "I hope that you'll be a better father than I was to you." These values are what we need to pass on to our next generation.

Teach your children well

One Texas teacher asked her group of Hispanic high school students, "Who do you want to be like when you grow up? All answered "I want to be white." Depending on the area you live in, your children may be uncomfortable with their identity. They may suffer from a low self-esteem and a lack of social bonding. These children need assurance and encouragement from parents.

In March 1994, the American Association for the Advancement of Science reported the homework habits of immigrant children from 77 countries. Their findings showed that on the average, immigrant children studied between 2 and 3 hours compared to only an hour a day for Americans. According to the report, the Asian immigrant children had the highest grade point average and spent the longest amount of time on homework.

Daily hours of homework	Grade Point Average
Less than 1 hour	2.02
1 to 2 hours	2.44
2 to 3 hours	2.75
3 or more	2.92

Among minorities, Asian children are known for their academic excellence. They aren't any smarter than Hispanic children. Yet Asian parents constantly express their high expectations to their children. Many of them tell their children that the sole reason for their coming to America was to give them a better education. Parental expectations could be a burden to some children, yet most of them get the message. They know their achievement will be the only way to honor their parents' sacrifice. They want to show their gratitude by meeting their parents' expectations. Children who respect their parents will not go astray.

Meanwhile, formal education is not everything. Your children will need values to live a meaningful life. *The Book of Virtues*, the best-seller by former Secretary of Education, William Bennett, lists some of the fundamental values parents can teach to their children: self-discipline, work [work ethic], honesty, compassion, courage, loyalty, responsibility, perseverance, faith, and friendship.

Now is the time for you to make an impact for children of all ages. The population of Hispanic teenage children 15-19 years old will rise 42 percent in the next ten years. This group of children is now in the 5-9 years old range, in their formative years, and waiting for teachers like you to make a difference in their lives. The best way to teach them is to be a role model yourself. When kids learn virtues in their childhood, they will have lifelong self-esteem. As the Bible says, "Train a boy in the way he should go; even when he is old, he will not swerve from it."

Encourage God's language

There is a growing movement toward bilingual education. Bilingual educators say that children lose a sense of individuality by becoming assimilated into public society.

Bilingual education is a scheme proposed in the late 1960s by Hispanic-American social activists. Later it was endorsed by a congressional vote. But is bilingual education in the best interests of our children?

Richard Rodriguez, in his book *The Hunger of Memory*, asserts that he has a right and an obligation to speak the public language of *los gringos* (white Americans). He argues further that separateness does not equal individuality and that full individuality is maintained by those who are able to consider themselves members of the crowd. Whether you are for or against bilingual education in public school, one thing is clear: if your children cannot speak English, their potential for success is limited in the global world.

English is not just the language of the United States. It's the universal language used in the international business world. In Singapore and Hong Kong, instructions are given in English in public schools. Korean and Japanese children start learning English in kindergarten. The Chinese start learning English in the womb: pregnant women play tapes so that the fetus has total immersion. The Chinese even adopt American names. They use names like Mary Ching or John Hsu. They believe that having an easy-to-use name helps them make friends in the world. They don't lose their cultural identity one bit. They don't deny themselves or lose self-esteem.

If your children already speak English, encourage them to speak Spanish. Linda Chavez, the author of *Out of the Barrio*, pointed out: "By the third generation in the US, a majority of Hispanics, like other ethnic groups, speak only English." Some Hispanic parents discourage Spanish at home out of fear that children may not adjust to the mainstream of society. Most children are perfectly capable of learning several languages at the same time. I have seen many Hispanic professionals who regret that their parents did not teach them Spanish. Corporations are now encouraging their executives, mostly white males, to learn a foreign language, especially Spanish, to make the best of NAFTA and Latin American markets.

Prepare your children well for the future and for heaven. "I speak Spanish to God, Italian to women, French to men, and German to my horse," said Charles V. Teach your children God's language.

Help thy neighbor

There is an old Mexican folk tale:

> A Mexican fisherman was collecting live crabs along the shore in an open bucket. A passerby stopped and asked, "Aren't you afraid those crabs will escape?" The fisherman replied, "There's no need to worry because these are Mexican crabs. As soon as one tries to move up to the top, the others bring him down."

Do these crabs have any resemblance to Hispanics? I hope not. When Henry Cisneros, Secretary of Housing and Urban Development, visited Los Angeles shortly after the devastating earthquake during January 1994, he came across many families living in Red Cross shelters. One whom he met was Alfred Arroyo, a car salesman with a wife and three children. Arroyo invited seventeen strangers in his make-shift tent to spend the night because they had no cover and the temperature was falling to a low of 47 degrees. He said making such a sacrifice was merely an extension of the tradition of *la posada* in Mexico, a celebration of the shelter given to Mary and Joseph in Bethlehem on the eve of Jesus' birth.

Hispanics have a long tradition of helping each other. Somehow, in the midst of the hustle and bustle of American life, we have lost some of those beautiful traditions. Hispanics need help from other Hispanics. Support Hispanic businesses if you can. Yet, do not blindly patronize them; help them improve. Make suggestions for them to excel in their businesses.

Many Hispanic children especially need your help. They will never know what opportunities exist outside the *barrio* or the housing projects. Reach out to them and give them hope. They need you to be their big brothers and sisters. They want you to be their counselors. Furthermore, reach out and touch their parents. You will plant the real seeds for reaping a better future. Our children's future and the future of the world depend on you.

Conclusion

Thank you for joining us by completing this book. This marks the end and sets a new beginning. Although our ancestors were among the first settlers in this country, it will be the 21st century that will note the Hispanic era in America. The new millennium will be marked with major Hispanic achievements. It is YOU that will MAKE the DIFFERENCE. The future of Hispanics and the future of America are in your hands:

- To restore strong values and virtues
- To move beyond survival to success
- To rekindle and realize the American Dream.

So let us start now.

Let us not see our image as others have seen us.
Instead, let us build a new image as we see ourselves.
With our new image, we will move forward as new leaders.

Act! Act! Act!
Let us not act out of fear.
And let us not fear to act.

With God as our guide, let us begin now.
Still dreaming, still achieving,
In each tomorrow, let us find that we're farther than today.

From the past we've learned
With future dreams to be earned,
Now is the time to become a New Hispanic, a new leader.

Notes to Yourself

- Write down your personal mission statement.

- Write down your goal and objectives for the next five years.

- Write down the image you need to develop to accomplish your goal.

- Write down your personal affirmations.

Appendix 1: Hispanic Achievers

Arts:
    Sandra Cisneros, author of *The House on Mango Street*
    Laura Esquivel, author of *Like Water for Chocolate*
    Gregory Mejia, artist
    Diego Peña, artist
    Richard Rodriguez, author of *The Hunger of Memory*

Business:
    Alfredo J. Estrada, Editor and Publisher, *HISPANIC* magazine
    Robert Goizueta, Chairman of the Board & CEO of Coca-Cola
    Steve Puente, Vice President of Employee Relations, Kraft General Foods
    Hector Ruiz, Senior Vice President, Paging Products Group, Motorola
    Sarah Martinez Tucker, Vice President, Consumer Communications Services, AT&T
    Joseph A. Unanue, President, Goya Foods

Entertainment:
    Gloria Estéfan, singer
    Andy Garcia, actor
    Tish Hinojosa, singer and guitarist
    Julio Iglesias, singer
    Tony Melendez, singer and guitarist
    Edward James Olmos, actor
    Paul Rodriguez, comedian and producer
    Linda Ronstadt, singer
    Christina Saralegui, syndicated talk show hostess
    Martin Sheen, actor

News Media:
    Giselle Fernandez, CBS News correspondent
    María Hinojosa, *Latino USA*, National Public Radio

Jackie Nespral, NBC co-anchor of *Weekend Today*
Elizabeth Vargas, NBC news correspondent
Jose Luis Ruiz, Executive Director, National Latino Communications Center

Government:
Henry Cisneros, Secretary of Housing and Urban Development
Kika de la Garza, (D-TX), Chairman of the House Agriculture Committee
Henry B. Gonzalez, (D-TX), Chairman of House Banking, Finance, and Urban Affairs Committee
Carmen Guzmán Lowry, Deputy Assistant for Congressional Affairs
Dan Morales, Texas Attorney General
Frederico Peña, Secretary of Transportation
Isabelle Rodriguez Tapia, Deputy Assistant to the President
Lucille Roybal-Allard, (D-CA), Vice-Chair of U.S. Congressional Hispanic Caucus
José Serrano, (D-NY), Chairman of U.S. Congressional Hispanic Caucus
Patti Solis, First Lady's Scheduler
Susanna A. Valdez, Associate Director for the White House Office of Public Liaison
Joe Velasquez, Deputy Assistant to the President

Science:
Louis Alvarez, scientist, Nobel Prize winner
Ellen Ochoa, NASA Astronaut

Sports:
Tony Casillas, football
Oscar De La Hoya, boxing
Gigi Fernandez, tennis
Juan Gonzalez, baseball
Tony Melendez, weightlifting
Chi Chi Rodriguez, golf
Alberto Salazar, running
Lee Treviño, golf
Fernando Valenzuela, baseball

Appendix 2: Suggested Reading

Ailes, Roger. *You are the Message*. New York: Doubleday, 1989.

Bennis, Warren. *On Becoming a Leader*. Reading: Addison-Wesley, 1989.

Brooks, Michael. *Instant Rapport*. New York: Warner Books, 1989.

Covey, Stephen. *The Seven Habits of Highly Effective People*. New York: Simon and Schuster, 1989.

Dilenschneider, Robert L. *Power and Influence: Mastering the Art of Persuasion*. New York: Prentice Hall, 1990.

Gracian, Baltasar. *The Art of Worldly Wisdom*. New York: Doubleday, 1992.

Korda, Michael. *Success!* New York: Ballentine Books, 1978.

Maltz, Maxwell. *Psycho-Cybernetics and Self-Fulfillment*. New York: Pocket Books, 1970.

Molloy, John. *Dress for Success*. New York: Warner Books, 1975.

Phillips, Linda and Wayne Phillips. *The Concise Guide to Executive Etiquette*. New York: Doubleday, 1990.

Sarnoff, Dorothy. *Never Be Nervous Again*. New York: Ballantine Books, 1989.

Steinem, Gloria. *Revolution from Within*. Boston: Little, Brown and Co., 1993.

Strunk, Jr., William and E.B. White. *The Elements of Style*. New York: Macmillan Publishing, 1979.

Sun-Tzu. *The Art of War*. Oxford, England: Oxford University Press, 1963.

Yate, Martin. *Knock'em Dead*. Holbrook, Mass: Bob Adams, 1991.

Also read the biographies of successful people including:

Bill Gates
Mikhail Gorbachev
John F. Kennedy

Madonna
James Michener
Akio Morita
Lee Iacocca
Michael Jordan
Jacqueline Kennedy Onassis
I. M. Pei
Rev. Robert Schuller
Norman Schwarzkopf
Margaret Thatcher
Barbara Walters
Sam Walton

About the Authors

Edward Valdez has spent more than a decade studying success principles of achievers around the world. Having personally experienced both success and failure, he is determined to share the lessons with other Hispanics and pave the road for their success. Prior to joining a Fortune 500 company, he had led more than 200 seminars and workshops on communication and personal marketing strategies. He is a *magna cum laude* graduate of the Massachusetts Institute of Technology with a B.S. in electrical engineering. Having received an MBA from the University of Texas at Austin, he serves on the Board of Directors of the National Society of Hispanic MBAs.

Dr. Kim Valdez is Executive Director of CEO International, a cross-cultural communication consulting and training firm in Austin, Texas. With a Ph.D. from the University of Texas at Austin, she has worked in the U.S. and overseas as a management/communication consultant. Her corporate clients include Fortune's Global 500 companies and her individual clients include top executives of multinational corporations. As an author of three books on image and communication, she is very much in demand as a speaker and has spoken to as many as 6,500 people in one day. She loves traveling around the world and finds joy in promoting cultural understanding.

Programs

CEO International, a cross-cultural communication consulting and training firm, offers seminars and workshops for Hispanic professionals. Topics include:

- Your cultural self-image
- Understanding cultural barriers
- Overcoming stereotypes
- Assessing your personal style
- Communicating across accents
- Speaking with authority
- Dress for success
- Body language and gestures
- Personal marketing strategies
- Presentation skills

Authors are available for speeches and seminars.

For more information, call (512) 343-0472 or fax (512) 343-8475.

To order additional copies of *New Hispanics* for yourself or for your friends:

> Please call 1-800-460-0300.
>
> In Austin, Texas, call 795-5000 (Austin only).

We Want Your Feedback

We are committed to improving the career paths of all Hispanics and need your help to do so. Please return your feedback about *New Hispanics* to us. You can make a copy of this page or tear it out. In return for your feedback, we will send you a free update of *New Hispanics*.

Which chapters were most valuable?

Which chapters were least valuable?

If you want to read another book on Hispanic career development, what new topics would you like to read about?

What are your suggestions for improving Hispanic professional success in America?

What are your suggestions for improving Hispanic images in America?

What are your experiences as a Hispanic professional in America?

Please send your feedback or comments to:
CEO International
P.O. Box 200902
Austin, Texas 78720-0902